Encounters

My Life in Publishing

Encounters

My Life in Publishing

by GEORGE BRAZILLER

George Braziller, Inc.
NEW YORK

"Grandpa, remember. You have only one chance to get it right."
Zachary Braziller

George Braziller, Inc.
277 Broadway, Suite 708
New York, NY 10007

Library of Congress Cataloging-in-Publication Data
Braziller, George, 1916–
Encounters : a memoir / by George Braziller.
    pages cm
ISBN 978-0-8076-0016-0
1. Braziller, George, 1916– 2. Publishers and publishing—New York (State)—New York—Biography. 3. George Braziller, Inc.—History. 4. Braziller, George, 1916—Friends and associates. 5. Authors and publishers—History—20th and 21st centuries. I. Title.

Z473.B794B73 2015
070.509747'1—dc23
                2014039359

Design and composition by Jason Burch

Printed and bound in China by Asia Pacific Offset

Contents

For Marsha

Preface

In 2011, at the age of ninety-five, after directing my publishing house for fifty-six years, I decided to turn over my affairs to my sons, Michael and Joel. It was a difficult decision. Publishing had been my entire life ever since my wife, Marsha, died in 1970.

Among the many mistakes I made, was not remarrying. I had a few opportunities, but always backed down, making some excuse or other. Naturally, I was attracted to lovely young women, but over the years always gave that same lame excuse: I am too old for you. That let me off the hook, but suddenly I found I *was,* in fact, too old. Then what? Solitude.

To my dismay and sorrow, a number of friends I had once partied and traveled with were now deceased. Making new friends was difficult. Still, I was physically limited in my movements, which presented problems. As much as I tried to make the best of my condition, I was withdrawing, although, as always, I enjoyed visiting museums and friends and doing volunteer work. I read a lot and, whenever I was able to get to a rally, I protested against the war in Afghanistan and against all war.

It was only after I had turned my publishing house over to my sons that I first considered writing a memoir. Discovering I had so much free time on my hands, my friends urged me to write about my life: "You have such a good story. Tell it!" they said—but I was not at all sure how good my story might be or if I were even capable of telling it.

At age ninety-five, I picked up Tolstoy's *War and Peace* for the very first time. I soon realized that I was holding in my hands what was perhaps the greatest novel written. I came upon the following passage in Clifton Fadiman's introduction:

We think of certain Tolstoyan scenes as other men would do them and then we realize the quality of his supremacy. Where coterie writers would use complex techniques, he uses the simplest. One can imagine what one of our smart young men would do with a scene like Andrew's delirium, cramming it full of Daliesque imagery and muddled streams of consciousness. Or take that great passage in which the daredevil Dolokhov balances himself on the window sill and drinks a bottle of rum on a bet. What subtle emotions that aren't really there he would put into it, what unnecessary underwriting, what overtones! But Tolstoy gives us only the scene itself, simply and vividly, yet with every desired effect obtained.

These comments about what it takes to be a writer inspired me with such a joyous feeling that I started to write my memoir. Perhaps I make starting sound easy. I found the process difficult. I felt that I wasn't a good writer, and writing came sporadically and painfully. I looked at every how-to book on writing. I bothered my friends for their support. When I did write, I often found I was too emotional to move forward on a steady course.

I learned something valuable, however, while reading *Specimen Days,* a collection of Walt Whitman's masterful notes, sketches, and essays. I learned to keep a record of the day's events. Every day, Whitman wrote whatever came to his mind—his observations, his feelings, and his thoughts. He wrote each day in a little notebook, and, in the end, there were hundreds of these notebooks.

I have tried to adopt Whitman's approach, to write my thoughts, memories, emotions, and observations simply and honestly. I feel fortunate that, at my age, I can express my innermost feelings by writing and raising eyebrows. I have found that writing helps me get through my solitude.

Part One

The Early Years

"Perhaps what one wants to say is formed in childhood and the rest of one's life is spent trying to say it."
— Barbara Hepworth

My mother and father

The Street

My parents, Rebecca and Joseph Braziller, emigrated from Russia to the United States in 1900, along with millions of others who were escaping hunger and religious persecution. They—and everyone else in the shtetl of Minsk—spoke only Yiddish. Friends greeted my parents at Ellis Island and took them to a three-room walk-up cold-water flat in East New York, a poor section of Brooklyn near the border with Queens. That flat at 456 Bradford Street would be the family home for the next thirty years.

From 1890 to 1916, my mother gave birth to seven children: two girls and five boys. I was the youngest, born on February 12, 1916. My father, who had been a garment worker in a sweatshop in Manhattan's Lower East Side, died of a lung tumor two months before I was born. My mother, my siblings, and I were packed into the small flat, which was stifling in summer and freezing in winter. We lived across from a neglected neighborhood playground, where I spent lots of time with my friends. World War I was still on, and the conditions for immigrants in a strange new land were discouraging. Still, my family considered itself lucky to have found a place to call home. My siblings and I spoke Yiddish before any of us learned to speak English.

My childhood memories of Brooklyn and East New York are of a place that is now long gone. Our family was just one of thousands of immigrant families that flooded New York with the hope of finding a better life, transforming the city's tenements and streets into miniature pockets of Europe. I grew up in what was called the ghetto, a five- or six-block area in Brownsville, a predominantly Jewish section of East New York. The streets of the marketplace were perpetually bustling with Polish, Italian, and Russian immigrants with pushcarts, selling everything imaginable: fruit and vegetables, meat and fish, clothes and hats and underwear. From her pushcart, my mother sold pants and old shoes.

As I walked out of our flat each morning, the air was filled with the voices of people shouting in Yiddish and every other conceivable foreign tongue. The din was indescribable. When words failed to save them a few pennies, customers bargained with their hands. Each evening, the streets overflowed with the debris of the day—cabbage leaves, broken eggs, half-eaten sour pickles, stray stockings, tattered yarmulkes—which was removed by street cleaners and scavengers.

The neighborhood block parties were great fun. They were held once or twice a year between Blake and Sutter avenues. It was wonderful to see families from different ethnic backgrounds come together to get to know each other for a few hours at least. Everyone smiled, showing a willingness to be friendly. They made brave attempts to communicate with sign language when words failed, which was more often than not.

The air was filled with the smells of so many different kinds of food that it was almost impossible to decide what to try first. There was a lot of guesswork before biting into strange foods we couldn't identify—and asking didn't help at all because we couldn't understand the answers. I remember tasting pizza for the first time at one of these block parties, but I tended to stick to what my mother had brought along—knishes and *creplach,* mostly.

During these block parties, there was a kind of unspoken truce among us kids. Normally, we avoided entering each other's turf at the risk of bloody noses. At these times, however, we put aside our street rivalries and enjoyed the party atmosphere. There was always plenty of food to take our minds off of our territorial differences. A few of us shook hands warily, looking away.

I recall very little about my sisters and brothers in the years before I met my "new" father at age eight. I never had the opportunity to learn much about them. My mother was out all day selling items from her pushcart, and my brothers and sisters had jobs away from home. When my sisters, Rose and Ida, were only twelve and thirteen years old, respectively, they found work as towel girls in a public bathhouse. They told my mother that both men and women would often grab at them. For fear of losing their jobs, however, they said nothing.

When I was not in school, I spent most of the day in the streets, playing with friends until dark or sitting on the stoop, waiting for someone to come home. I was afraid of being alone in the empty flat. A kid named David Kaminsky (who later become famous as Danny Kaye) lived in the neighborhood. I sometimes spotted him at the corner drugstore where I hung out, although we never spoke. A born entertainer, he was then already singing comic songs and improvising dance steps.

During those childhood days, the seasons never mattered—they were fluid and only signaled a switch in the type of street games we played. In the summer, we opened the hydrants and played under the cooling spray that sparkled with the colors of the rainbow. In winter we built enormous snowmen and snow forts. I loved the evenings, when the streetlights went on, casting shadows everywhere. One of our made-up games was posing as famous people, mostly baseball players and actors. My favorite character to play was Charlie Chaplin. I didn't have a battered derby for my head, but I enjoyed imitating his walk.

Fridays were special. I would return from school without detouring for a game of punch ball with my friends. I hurried home to clean up our flat before my mother returned. I would wash the floors and dust the table. I would prepare the kitchen table for supper, although I don't remember any fancy dinnerware. My mother usually arrived at dusk. I would wait for her on the street corner, rushing to meet her to take the heavy bags she was carrying, which were full of the items she had been unable to sell.

I loved to watch my mother at the stove. If she had had a good day with the pushcart, there would be fish or chicken for dinner. If she had had a bad day, it would be potato soup with gizzards, bitter sour pickles, and herring. Before she began cooking, she would look around the flat, call me over, and give me a kiss, saying *Zer schön, zer gut* ("Very nice, very nice"). Soon after eating, everyone would fall into bed, dead tired. Yet, as tired as she was, before we went to sleep, my mother would always tell us stories of what it was like in Russia when she was a girl. Her stories were in Yiddish, but my sisters, who had learned English, would jokingly tease her. "Speak English! Speak English!" they urged her.

Our flat was heated only with a coal stove, which required constant fueling with coal or wood scraps. The only way to keep warm was to sit close to the stove. We bought ice from a wagon to preserve food in our icebox. The block of ice lasted only a day or two, depending on how hot the days were. When the nights were very cold, I crept into bed with my sisters. I loved their sweet smell and warmth and gradually fell asleep. In winter, school was the only place where we could be warm most of the day.

By the age of seven, I had already developed an entrepreneurial streak. The tenants on the floor of our building shared the common toilet down the hall—a typical arrangement in tenement housing. Because nearly everyone had to use the facilities at the same time each morning, I discovered a way to make a few extra pennies. When the toilet was available, I knocked on the doors of the good tippers to alert them that they should hurry to take occupancy. I showed favoritism to the parents of one of the little girls I had a crush on.

Everyone who lived in the crowded tenements tried to find ways to overcome the claustrophobic conditions. In hot weather, people climbed up to the roof with their bedding to try to get some sleep. By the end of summer, the entire neighborhood ended up there. The Jews congregated in their own corner of the roof, and the Italians and Poles in theirs, so there was very little intermixing. Young people danced to records on the gramophone, and children played until they dropped off to sleep from exhaustion. My mother didn't tell me stories on the roof, but she softly hummed Yiddish folk songs as I gazed up at the darkening blue sky.

Privacy was not highly valued in our neighborhood. No one had a private telephone. The only telephone in the area was located at the corner drug store, where you waited in line to enter the booth and slide the door shut. The rest of the people waiting in line would strain to overhear conversations. Some people cheated the phone company by inserting flattened pennies, instead of nickels, into the slots to pay for their calls.

Just two blocks from Bradford Street was Public School 142, which I attended from ages five to seven. One of my sisters, either Ida or Rose, walked me there each morning. The teacher gave me a couple of primers, which I didn't know how to read. Rose helped me with them. I loved looking at picture books, although the words meant nothing.

We lived close to the neighborhood of Canarsie, where, during the

Blake Avenue

1920s, descendants of the original Dutch settlers were still farming. I loved the sounds of the Dutch street names: Van Sicklen, Van Sinderen. I would accompany my mother to Canarsie to buy fresh milk. I loved the taste of the warm milk and loved watching the cows standing in the barn so patiently. The Dutch farmers allowed me to roam around the farm. The air felt different there—fresher, like walking into a park. I liked these farmers very much. They often gave us a few eggs and potatoes to take home.

I remember being happy when my aunt, Mimmi (the word *mimmi* means "aunt" in Yiddish, so I simply called her that), came over to read the Yiddish newspaper, the *Jewish Daily Forward,* aloud to my mother. I remember seeing a photograph of Franklin Delano Roosevelt in one of her newspapers, so I just assumed he was Jewish.

On the rare occasions when my mother wasn't working, she took me and my brothers—Charles, Ben, Michael, and Sam—by train to Coney Island. There, we enjoyed the famous Nathan's hot dogs with plenty of mustard and sauerkraut. Those hot dogs cost only a nickel, as did almost everything else at Coney Island then: the train fare, the Ferris wheel, the rides and games at Luna Park.

Once, my brother Sam tried to teach me how to swim by holding me down under the water for several minutes, which seemed like an eternity to me. Perhaps he thought everyone learned to swim that way. He finally let me come up for air when he realized I was swallowing a lot of salt water and was half-drowned. After swimming, I always wanted to go with my mother into the women's section of the bathhouse to change out of my bathing suit, but, smiling, she pushed me toward the men's section.

At age eight, I was heartbroken when Ida and Rose left home to share a room somewhere. "Where are they going? Aren't they ever coming back?" I tearfully asked my mother.

Today I recall with amazement and admiration how my mother, alone after my father's death, was able to live in that three-room flat, raise seven children, and sell clothing from a pushcart all day, during the bitter years of the First World War and the Great Depression. This memoir is a tribute to her—my dear mother, whom I loved so much.

Huntington Station

One day, when I was eight years old, my mother and I were looking at some picture books. There was a knock at the door. In walked a man whom I had never seen before. I was frightened. I can't recall ever seeing strangers in our flat. I hid behind my mother and watched as she and the man embraced.

My mother said, "Son, meet your new father." My father had died before I was born, and I had never heard the word "father" before—nor did I understand its meaning. I burst out crying, calling for my sisters, Rose and Ida. I ran out of the room and into a closet.

The next week, my mother, stepfather, and I moved to Huntington Station, on the north shore of Long Island. My stepfather, Jacob Gross, had lived there before he married my mother. He planned to work with his brother and my mother in a tailor shop.

During the trip to Huntington Station, the whistle of the Long Island Rail Road steam locomotive sounded scary to a lonely boy. When I asked my mother where we were going, she put her arm around me and said we were going to our new home. I said I liked the home we had and liked the playground and my friends. I asked what was wrong with where we were living. She held me tightly and wept, but didn't answer.

At the time, Huntington Station, where we would live for the next seven years, was a rural village surrounded by farms. It was nothing like the prosperous community it is today. Many of the roads were unpaved, and street lighting had not yet been completely installed. I often went out at night to look at the sky full of stars, hoping to see a shooting star. Several Jewish families had already moved into the area and opened stores on the main street. I learned later that Walt Whitman had been born in nearby West Hills. (Today there is a shopping mall named after him on a main north-to-south artery. His birthplace still stands as an historic site.)

The Huntington Station public school was located about a mile away from our house on a lovely hill surrounded by trees. I still couldn't read English very well, although I spoke it well enough. Just as they did in my Brooklyn school, the kids in my class made fun of my accent.

Huntington Station

When I did learn to read English more fluently, I read *The Pickwick Papers* by Charles Dickens. The stories were funny, and the characters so real. At age ten, I began to deliver newspapers in the morning before school started. I was often so tired I fell asleep at my desk. Still, on my report cards, my average grade was B.

The seating in the classrooms was arranged alphabetically by surname. As mine was Braziller, I was seated up front, close to the teacher's desk. The teacher's name was Miss O'Brien, and she made me as uncomfortable as possible every chance she got.

Miss O'Brien was young and beautiful and she was also a good teacher. She was very helpful to us kids, but she seemed to take a funny sort of pleasure in calling on me to stand and answer questions when I would have been better off remaining seated. By age eleven, I was beginning to feel the stirrings of manhood, which manifested itself with embarrassingly regular erections that Miss O'Brien could clearly see from her desk. When I stood to answer her question, I squirmed into every conceivable position to conceal my erection, which was only as large as one could expect in a young boy but was obviously visible to her.

When we lived in Brooklyn, my mother loved to socialize. In

Huntington, very few people spoke Yiddish, and she was lonely. So, in the evenings, I began to walk my mother to classes where she and several other people from the local synagogue learned to speak and read English. After classes, she and I practiced together.

My mother eventually became an American citizen and was very eager to vote for FDR in the 1932 election. When she went to the polls on Election Day, she received instant approval to register because she was able to show a note from her English instructor saying she had had a perfect attendance record. When she received the approval to vote, she broke out in tears, repeating, "Thank you, thank you."

When I was twelve, my mother wanted very much for me to be bar mitzvahed. She was no more observant than many other members of the local synagogue, but she insisted that I take religious instruction from the local rabbi, Rabbi Herman, and prepare myself for the initiation into manhood. I read the Torah with Rabbi Herman three afternoons a week—for many boring and tiring weeks—and became adept at speaking Hebrew. When the big day came for the ceremony at the synagogue, my mother, who sat in the balcony behind a white curtain with the other women, was ecstatic. I and the other boys had to read from the Torah and proclaim to the congregation, "Today I am a man."

As each young "man" left the platform with the Rabbi's blessing, he received a fountain pen from his proud mother and father. I didn't receive a pen—we didn't have the money, and I didn't have a father. My stepfather was at home, ill. "Mama, Mama, I didn't get a fountain pen." I was so disappointed that I ran crying from the synagogue.

Years later, when I told this story to my friend, the English author Beryl Bainbridge, she laughed and said, "Poor George." A week later, a package arrived from Beryl, in which I found a beautiful fountain pen with a note that read, "Dear George, today you are a man." I have repeated this story to several others since then, and today I am drowning in fountain pens. I have since stopped telling the story.

My teenage years in Huntington Station were reasonably happy, but, for the most part, they were wasted. I just drifted. Most of my friends were older than I was. Some had jobs, and some had gone on to college.

My school, 1928

The best I could do with my limited education was to work as a golf caddy or on local farms. My stepfather died, I was fifteen, so I tried to help my mother however I could.

Somehow, I had the same feeling in Huntington Station that I had had in East New York: a feeling of emptiness at the end of each day. There was no one to ask me, "What did you do today?" or "What did you learn today?" or anyone to tell me what was right or what was wrong. There was no one with whom I could share my feelings, which I can only describe as feelings of desolation. In Huntington, I learned to miss a father.

When my mother said to me one day, "We are going back to Brooklyn to live," I was happier than I had been in a long time, although I would miss my friends and the times spent in Huntington.

My First Dance

My first dance was for my graduation from junior high school, at age fifteen. Initially I didn't want to go, as I didn't have anything decent to wear. I cried about this for days. Finally my mother managed to put an outfit together for me so I could go to the dance.

I wanted to look good for the dance and thought a suntan would put some color in my pale face. One hot summer's day, I went to the beach in Huntington Harbor, stretched out on the sand, and fell asleep. Of course, when I woke up my skin was on fire. I began to feel a lot of pain, especially later, while getting dressed in my new clothes, which brushed against my skin.

I almost didn't go to the dance, but my mother pushed me. The dance was in our school gymnasium. Most of my classmates were there. Parents stood along the left and right walls, and teachers stood along the back. I walked over to my classmate, Elizabeth Dorner, bowed, and asked her to dance. When the band played the song, "Goodnight, Sweetheart," I was happy, despite my painful sunburn. The pain didn't matter. I was holding in my arms my first love. If you had listened closely, you would have heard me humming, "Goodnight, sweetheart."

Me and the black Buick

Alpacuna

The early 1930s were among the most difficult years of my life. I was about sixteen. At different times, I lived with different brothers and sisters, some of whom were married. I was happy just to have a place to sleep. We all struggled during the years of the Great Depression. I did my best not to be a burden to them, so I took any job I could find. I spent most of my time walking the same streets, again and again, looking for work, which was damned hard to find.

My brother's friend, Ben, got me a job as a salesman's assistant. The salesman was named Nat Tepper. It was the first decent job I had ever had.

Nat Tepper represented a prestigious clothing company from Philadelphia. His chief product was an extraordinary coat called the Alpacuna, which Tepper said was made of camel hair. I didn't know what he was talking about and was astounded when he said the coat sold for $100. I thought he was fooling around.

During my interview, Tepper told me that I was lucky. I had the right height, was not bad looking, and had a good figure for the job. I was to model Tepper's coats for stores and customers. Tepper would pay for all my meals and hotel rooms and give me seven dollars a week.

I jumped at the chance. The opportunity to see New England was exciting (I had never been out of New York), and it was great not to have to worry about where my next meal was coming from.

While driving me around in his big black Buick, Tepper talked a great deal, often about sex. He said he was going to educate me and take care of me (I was still a virgin). He bragged how in every city he had someone waiting for him at a hotel. I laughed. I thought he was making it up.

I enjoyed the job and the car rides. We would stop somewhere, and Tepper would call on one of his customers. I would model the coats—a few jokes then from Tepper, and the sale was made. I marveled at Tepper's skill as a salesman. I was always wishing I could own one of those Alpacunas.

When we got to Boston, we checked into separate hotel rooms.

A little while later, Tepper came in and told me that he had arranged someone for me. He told me what to do, handed me five dollars and a rubber, and left. A very nice young girl walked in, said hello, and undressed beside the bed. I was terribly nervous. I asked her questions—what her name was, if she liked what she did. The whole time she was just standing there naked, looking at me. I was still dressed.

Suddenly she put her clothes back on and said, "Five bucks. Your time is up." Tepper came back in and asked, "How did it go, George?" I handed him the rubber and said, "Great!"

When we got back to New York, my work for Tepper, sadly, came to an end. We joked around as we said good-bye. Tepper asked if I wanted anything. I looked at him and replied, "An Alpacuna." Tepper didn't give me an Alpacuna, but he gave me some money and a handshake.

I often think about Tepper. He was like a big brother to me. I envied his life as a salesman, traveling to new places and meeting new people (and having lots of sex).

The Spanish Civil War

While we were still living in Huntington, my stepfather died of cancer. I was fifteen. My mother and I then moved back to Brooklyn. My mother lived with my sister Rose, and I rented a room on Blake Avenue in East New York, quite close to where I had grown up. I was happy to be back with my siblings and neighborhood friends again.

One day I remember the shouts of people drawing me to a street rally on Sutter Avenue. The speaker was perched on a flag-decked ladder. I didn't understand much of what he was saying, but I heard people young and old shouting "war," and "Spain" and "Hitler."

Afterward, as the crowd milled about, I felt a tap on my shoulder. I turned, and there was the speaker. He was a bit taller than I was and had a pleasant face. He held out his hand and said, "Hi, my name is Mike Lederman. Do you live around here?" "No," I replied, wanting to get away. I didn't want to get involved. "What do you think of what I said?" he asked. I mumbled a word or two. He handed me a sheet of paper with text and photos and said, "Read this, kid. If you wish, you can come to the meeting tomorrow and hear about everything." I mumbled once again, took the paper, and made my getaway.

Back in my room I read the flyer's headline: "Spain Begs for Help! 3/16/1938." It was a report on Hitler and Mussolini's support of General Francisco Franco in the Spanish Civil War. German planes were bombing Madrid and Toledo and had destroyed the village of Guernica. "If you want to help the Spanish people," the text read, "come to the next meeting." It gave the time and address.

At the time, the world news in the paper meant very little to me. I had never heard about this civil war. I was young. I was thinking mainly about finding a job or about whether Joe Louis would win his next fight or where my next meal might come from. Having nothing else to do, I decided to attend the meeting.

The room was filled with mostly young men and women of all ages. They cheered or booed in response to what the speakers shouted. Several people asked me who Hitler and Mussolini were. Europe seemed very far away to everyone. I knew very little, but we talked and tried to learn from each other. There were banners and flags with written slogans supporting the Republic of Spain against Franco's Nationalist forces. Posters demanded the freedom of the Spanish poet, Federico García Lorca. (I could not imagine then that thirty-six years later, I would publish a biography of this great poet.)

So I gradually discovered the world of politics. I began attending protest groups in support of the Spanish Loyalists. I joined the Young Communist League. I organized meetings and agitated in the streets. I was arrested once, but was released the following day—all of which gave me a feeling of great importance.

I remember a huge political rally held at Madison Square Garden when the Spanish people's cause was looking grim. The Garden was filled with more than 20,000 people. They went wild when Ernest Hemingway was introduced. Hemingway's appearance gave the audience the support it needed.

I was fired with enthusiasm that the Loyalists would succeed. I was cheered by the fact that prominent artists, writers, and musicians from all over America lent their support to the Republican cause in Spain—Hemingway, Dorothy Parker, Paul Robeson, and John Dos Passos among them. Many of the Americans who managed to join the Abraham Lincoln Battalion got to Spain by way of Canada and France. There were also many Frenchmen and Englishmen who joined the fighting, including André Malraux and George Orwell.

In 1938, I joined the volunteer battalion, but the U.S. State Department denied my passport application. I was told that it was illegal for Americans to fight for a foreign nation and was threatened with a jail sentence. (After World War II, I was denied a passport again—even though I was a veteran—because of my activities during the Spanish Civil War. I eventually got a passport years later, during the Truman administration.)

I continued my activities in support of the Spanish Republic until the Loyalists' defeat in 1939. It was not hard to see the threat of a general conflict throughout Europe. At that time, I was working as a shipping

THAT SPAIN'S CHILDREN MAY LIVE

GIVE! SPANISH AID WEEK
MAY 30TH TO JUNE 9TH
NORTH AMERICAN COMMITTEE
TO AID SPANISH DEMOCRACY
NATIONAL OFFICE: 381 FOURTH AVENUE, NEW YORK

That Spain's Children May Live   Poster   1937

clerk, making fifteen bucks a week. During my hours off, I pounded on doors, begging people who didn't have much money to help the Republicans in Spain. Spain might as well have been on the moon. I tried to describe the brutalities of the Franco regime as best as I could. Some people listened politely. Others slammed the door in my face.

Only in retrospect do I understand the impact that the Spanish Civil War had on me. At its start in 1936, no one knew much about the war, nor could they foresee its ramifications. Shaped by the political education I received during these troubled times, I learned to see the world through other people's eyes.

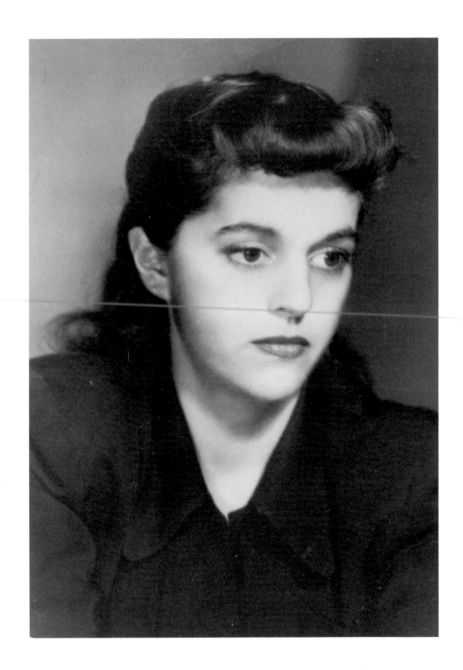

Marsha

I met Marsha Nash around 1934 or 1935, when I was about eighteen or nineteen. She was two years younger than I was. We were both living in Brooklyn. I was in East New York, working as a shipping clerk, living in a furnished room for five dollars a month. Marsha worked as a dental assistant and lived with her family in Cypress Hills, an area close to the border of Brooklyn and Queens.

I had seen Marsha occasionally in a local bookstore that carried mainly left-wing literature. You could browse there for hours without feeling obliged to buy anything. I used to spend time there enjoying the latest titles, usually without purchasing a thing. It's a mystery how the shop survived as long as it did.

The bookstore gained some notoriety when Alfred Kazin, a well-known Brooklyn-born writer and author of *A Walker in the City,* began to drop in. He sometimes would read to whomever happened to be present. I was impressed by Kazin's knowledge of politics and world affairs. He was only a year older than I was, yet he projected his arguments with admirable ease and confidence. I liked him even when he teased me about my rigid position on Communism.

One day when I was in the store, I spoke to Marsha. It was a challenge, as I was shy. She was about five foot seven, with large dark eyes set in a beautiful oval face. She reminded me of the actress Bette Davis. She had lovely, perfect teeth and spoke almost theatrically. She avoided facing people directly, as though she couldn't wait to move on. From head to toe, I thought she was a work of art—her laughter, her smile, her stance, her arms and hands, constantly expressing her thoughts.

A student at Thomas Jefferson High School, Marsha wrote poetry and worked after school hours. After graduating, she decided not to write poetry any longer—something I have always regretted. She always enjoyed a good laugh, sometimes at her own expense. We were married in 1936 and had two sons: Michael and Joel (whose nickname was Jimmy).

When Marsha and I got married, we were very young. We hardly knew each other. In 1943, I left to serve in World War II. When I came back after two years in the army, we had to get to know each other all over again.

At the age of forty, I worried that I was at the end of living. In my work, I met a lot of women and started to pay more attention to them than to Marsha. It was just like Marsha to put up with my womanizing, to give me the necessary time she thought I would need to pull out of it.

When she was dying, at the age of fifty-one, our sons, Jimmy and Michael, and I were with her in the hospital. She looked at Jimmy. Her last words were, "Did you have lunch yet?" She didn't even look at me. It was a real blow to me, as I deserved. I have lived with that memory ever since.

The Book Find Club

My start in the book world came when I was working during the dreary years of the Great Depression as a fifteen-dollar-a-week shipping clerk at Remainder Book Company. Marsha and I were recently married and we lived in a fifteen-dollar-a-month basement apartment. I was about twenty years old.

My "generous" brother-in-law, Morris Sorkin, owned Remainder. After a year there I was still just a shipping clerk, still learning how to tie up a book package properly. When I asked for a one-dollar raise, Morris refused. He really was a nice guy—but he never liked the way I tied up a book package.

I thanked Morris for giving me the opportunity to work and said good-bye. I didn't know what I would do next, and it seemed like a long walk home. I had to break the news to my wife, Marsha.

When I walked through the apartment door, I didn't waste much time. I said, straight out, "Marsha, I quit my job." I sat down and waited. Marsha was wonderful. She said, "I'm still working, and we'll manage."

Work of any kind was not easy to find in those days, especially for a dropout with only two years of high school. Leaving that job encouraged me to start out on my own.

I had heard about a book club in England called the Left Book Club. I was also aware of the Book-of-the-Month Club, an American club that was very successful and influential, distributing to thousands of subscribers. The publisher Doubleday also had its own club, the Literary Guild.

I eventually began to think seriously about starting a club of my own, which I would call the Book Find Club. I thought I could appeal to students and to a working-class audience, selling selections at affordable prices—say, two dollars a month, or less when practicable. One of my first titles was *Seeds of Liberation* by John Hyde Preston. I bought ten copies from the Remainder Book Company for twenty-five cents each and sold them to my subscribers for fifty cents each. Suddenly I was in business.

I worked seven days a week to get the club on its feet, recruiting subscribers from among family and friends. The first subscriber was Marsha, who paid with fifty cents and a kiss. I visited union halls, parent organizations, and teacher groups to talk up the book club. Luckily, I was welcomed everywhere. Many people promised to take one book a month.

My biggest expense in running the Book Find Club was renting office space for shipping. I rented space on Irving Place in Manhattan. My first employee was Herman Figatner, a young man with experience in the mail-order business. He remained not only a trusted employee but also a beloved friend for more than fifty years.

One of Book Find's most important selections was *Under Cover* by John Roy Carlson, issued in 1943. It was an exposé of the Nazi underworld in the United States during World War II. Carlson named names. There were several attempts to sabotage the distribution of *Under Cover*. All of them were unsuccessful, I am happy to say.

The Book Find Club grew because of the quality of the selections and authors—and the low prices—which brought in thousands of new subscribers. These are some of our titles: *The Basic Writings of Thomas Paine; The Naked and the Dead* by Norman Mailer; *Tobacco Road* by Erskine Caldwell; *Wide Is the Gate* by Upton Sinclair; and *The Age of Jackson* by Arthur Schlesinger Jr.

From 1943 through the early 1950s, the Book Find Club was very successful, enrolling thousands of new members. We soon had a membership of 100,000. The Club became a force, distributing what many considered to be thoughtful, "liberal," "left-wing" books—by authors such as those mentioned above and Arthur Miller.

The height of our success coincided with the beginnings of what came to be known as the Red Scare, the blacklisting that took place from 1950 to 1956, during the era of McCarthyism. Thousands of our members called into our office or arrived in person, begging that we destroy their membership cards, hysterical with fear that they would be accused of being Communists, afraid they would be blacklisted and lose their jobs. What could I do? Of course, our hearts went out to these

Herman Figatner and me

frightened people. Due to the terror of the McCarthy Era, the Book Find Club membership dropped to 50,000. Sadder for me was the thought that often came to me during the night that I was somehow responsible for those people's hardships.

I was so exhausted after working at the business for almost 20 years. I was eager to start my own publishing company. Later, I sold the Book Find Club to Time-Life for a considerable sum of money. By the time of the sale, we had built the club membership back up to 100,000—and it was still growing. Time-Life folded the club about two years later. We never understood why.

Richard Seaver

Dick Seaver came to work for me as the editor of my two book clubs: Book Find and Seven Arts. At the time, I was mostly interested in running the publishing house, for many reasons, including my vanity. I found publishing more exciting after having already run the book clubs for almost 20 years.

Seaver was inexperienced and needed time to learn the job. As he wrote in his memoir, *The Tender Hour of Twilight,* he was overwhelmed while trying to learn the book club business. Although he had full support from others on the staff, the job Dick had was very challenging. At the time, I was under a lot of pressure myself—trying to start a publishing company while keeping the book clubs going. Because of my own stress, I was often impatient with Dick and, at times, even rude to him.

One day, he was so angry with me that he came into my office and finally told me off. After that we became the best of friends—although I must admit that I don't think I fully deserved his friendship, given the way I had sometimes treated him.

Barney Rosset, the publisher of Grove Press, had heard about Seaver and his skills as an editor. After Dick had been with Braziller for two years, Rosset took him away from our publishing house. Perhaps one of the biggest mistakes I made in my publishing house was losing Dick. Had we kept him, we might have had some of the many great writers he worked with—including Jean Genet, Samuel Beckett, and Henry Miller. But Dick taught me a valuable lesson about how to deal with people.

Part Two

The War

"I think that there is, in the heroic courage with which man confronts the irrationality of the world, a beauty greater than the beauty of art."
— W. Somerset Maugham

World War II

With World War II going full blast, in 1943, shortly after the birth of our first son, I was drafted into the army, along with hundreds of thousands of other American boys. My good friends, Mike and Mac (like me, married men with children), were also drafted. We were all sent to Camp Upton in Yaphank, Long Island, but later were assigned to different regiments. Mike was killed at Anzio, and Mac was killed somewhere else in Italy.

While I was away, Marsha would carry on the Book Find Club, with the help of our good friend and treasurer, Herman Figatner. At the time, the club had 20,000 members and quite a few employees. I gave a little farewell talk to everyone on staff about how Germany and Japan were challenging our precious freedoms, including the freedom to print and read books. I asked them to do all they could to help Marsha and keep the Book Find Club afloat until I returned, if I returned.

133d AAA Gun Battalion with author circled

Boot Camp

After leaving Camp Upton, we spent ten days at Camp Shanks in Orangetown, New York. To see how we recruits might fit into army life, we received routine physical examinations, got a few shots, and answered questions about our civilian experiences and the foreign languages we spoke. As part of our final indoctrination into the U.S. Army, we all did KP ("kitchen patrol") duty, swept and mopped the barracks, kept our clothes in order, and did all the dull, boring things one does in boot camp. We also got to know each other.

After the difficult ten days we spent at Camp Shanks, it was a relief finally to be sent to Camp Edwards, located on Cape Cod. We arrived at Camp Edwards, eager for any change of scenery.

Many of the men in my outfit were from the New York area. The best thing was getting our weekend passes to New York. We were also allowed to receive visits from our wives and sweethearts at the camp. If we didn't have enough time to go into New York, we went to the nearby town of Buzzards Bay to get a few drinks, socialize with women, and simply get away from the deadening army routine.

Boot camp and basic training were difficult, but I learned a lot from the experience. Men from all over the country and from all walks of life had to learn to live and work together and tolerate each other's ways and beliefs. We also had to learn to care for each other. We realized that our lives might be in the hands of our buddies—and their lives might be in ours—and that the only way an army can *work* is if the men *work together*.

(It's strange to read what I've just written, coming from one who has always been such a hotheaded pacifist.)

Going Overseas

At 9:30 a.m., July 24, 1944, we were on our way—officers and soldiers of every rank. We were eager to have a last sorrowful look at the States from on board ship. With so many guys rushing to the side for a look, it seemed as though the ship might roll over.

To our left we could see the Ferris wheel at Coney Island, where I had spent many happy days with my mother, brothers, and sisters. I could still taste those Nathan's hot dogs, with mustard and sauerkraut. To our right we could see the Statue of Liberty, which had welcomed millions of immigrants to this country. The statue was now saying farewell to our boys, many of whom would never return.

Our ship, the *Mauretania,* was a former luxury liner that had been converted into a troop carrier. There were about 15,000 soldiers jammed into every available space—when standing, sitting, sleeping, showering, walking, and eating. The ocean crossing to England was peaceful, and the weather calm, but, still, the ship bounced around in the water like an enormous cork. Almost everyone—including me—was seasick for long periods of time.

We spent as much time on deck as possible. We liked the fresh air. We played poker, blackjack, and dice. Sometimes we just talked or read books, mostly paperbacks, which were given out for free. There were books by Ernest Hemingway, William Faulkner, and Agatha Christie. It was during this time that I discovered Walt Whitman. I carried a paperback book of his poetry in my duffel bag. We passed the time dreaming and wondering what lay ahead of us. Thoughts of loved ones began to recede.

On our third day out of New York Harbor, I heard a call over the loudspeakers, asking for volunteers to work in the library. "Gosh," I thought, "this is for me!" I shot up my hand and was told to report below deck, to Cabin A. Well, it turned out that Cabin A was the kitchen, and I was on KP duty. One thing I never managed to learn about the U.S. Army was never to volunteer for *anything.*

After three or four days in the North Atlantic, we glimpsed the shore of Ireland on the misty horizon and we knew our voyage was finally nearing its end. There was a lot of cheering and yelling. A few of the boys started singing, "The Yanks are coming, the Yanks are coming." It was a proud and thrilling moment.

As we drew close to England, Liverpool came into view. We were angry to see what had happened to the great city. There was devastation everywhere: blown-up gas tanks, torn-apart homes, uprooted trees. The city was in utter chaos and ruin. It looked as though the Germans had just left. I could not help but think about my family, safe back home, and hoped that the war would quickly come to an end.

Disembarking took almost half a day, as thousands of soldiers, loaded down with gear and weapons, tried to leave the ship all at the same time. When we were finally off, we fell into formation. We were driven to the town of Macclesfield, a staging area where we would receive all our equipment and further training in preparation for our eventual landing in German-occupied France.

On the morning of August 19, we rolled into Dorset County, the starting point for D-Day, the June 6 invasion of Normandy. We were assigned to Camp Marabout, outside of Dorchester. I couldn't help thinking about the thousands of soldiers from our camp who had already left for France, to be among the first soldiers to cross the English Channel and storm the beaches to gain a foothold for the Allies.

Our Dock Landing Ship (LSD) was out in the Channel on the way to France when we were hit by a fierce storm. Our ship was one of ten LSDs in formation in the Channel. We all had to head back and wait for the weather to clear up. The maneuver of turning around was itself dangerous because we were sitting ducks for the Germans. While we were turning around, side by side, bumping into each other, their submarines could have attacked us at any time.

When our ship landed in France, we saw nothing but German and Allied wreckage scattered everywhere along the beach.

I was a private in the 133d AAA Gun Battalion. We were assigned to defend a large tract of land that had the code name Omaha Beach. We set up our guns high on a hill. As I looked out at the hills of France, I was struck with fear for the first time. We knew that the Germans had built their concrete pillboxes and were waiting for us. During the month of September, we protected vital installations as the Germans retreated. On September 30, we assumed the new role of air and seacoast defense for the port of Cherbourg. Our duties included firing our 90-mm antiaircraft guns at the German V-1 flying "buzz" bombs that were headed directly for London.

On Christmas Eve, we heard the sound of a terrific explosion out in the Channel. A German submarine had torpedoed an American troop ship. Hundreds of boys had abandoned ship and were floundering in the water.

Our officers ordered every available boat out to help with the rescue, but many of the men were already past helping. We made every effort to save the wounded. We were all instructed to get to the hospital to give blood. There was utter chaos in spite of everyone's best efforts. Over the next few days, we heard the sad news that many boys didn't make it.

The winter of 1944–1945 was bitterly cold. I was still stationed in Cherbourg, a lowly private in the U.S. Army. The days dragged on and on—rain, snow, and constant cold. When we first arrived in France, we had hoped we would be stationed near a big city—with cafes, entertainment, and women. No such thing. American soldiers were not welcome.

There were some small means of escape. Once a week, we got six-hour passes. It was a great relief to get away from our rain-soaked quarters, and we naturally headed for where the action was. A barn was set aside so we could have all the sex we could buy from the local women. I recall the first time I was to have sex with a prostitute and how I talked myself out of it at the crucial moment. The guys next in line threatened to blow up the barn if I didn't finish up and get the hell out of there.

Finally, on New Year's Day, the move everyone had been hoping for happened. In the early hours we left Cherbourg—without regret— and sped east to the more cheerful atmosphere of the Champagne region. We craned our necks from the rear of trucks to catch a fleeting glimpse of the Eiffel Tower and the Seine. By mid-afternoon, snow still falling, we arrived in the historic and attractive city of Reims. For the first time in a long time, we had showers, hot food, and warm, dry beds. Best of all, we had passes to Paris.

In Paris we were greeted as heroes. Young women rushed up and kissed us. A few American flags flew from windows and balconies. The Parisians gave us drinks and food, and they never asked us for money. It was quite a different welcome from the one we had received in Cherbourg just a short time before.

One day, while we were in Reims, a voice bellowed over the loudspeaker, "Fall out!" We all rushed to where we were supposed to muster. There was a call for volunteers to go to Belgium. The Battle of the Bulge was raging there. The American G.I.s, surrounded by the Germans, were taking heavy losses.

As is my way, I shot my arm up impulsively. I still had not learned *never* to volunteer for *anything* in the U.S. Army. In the following days, as I and the dozen others who had volunteered were packing up to go to Belgium, I wondered why I had volunteered. Was I really a brave man or just a show-off? Back home, I had a wife and child who might be widowed and orphaned. Was I being responsible? It was too late to back out. Fortunately, the mission was called off two days later, and although I felt relieved, I was ashamed that I felt relieved. Tens of thousands of American boys fought and died at the Bulge, the largest and bloodiest battle of World War II.

The 133d AAA
GUN BATTALION

✶ ✶ ✶

About the Book

When the war with Germany ended in May 1945, I was stationed in Austria, still a private in the 133rd AAA Gun Battalion. I had been away from home for more than two years. When Germany surrendered, I thought we would be quickly discharged and sent home. No such luck. As the days, weeks, and months dragged on, I looked forward to my own liberation. The army kept us busy with boring minor duties, endless drilling and cleaning of equipment.

One day, I approached Lieutenant Colonel John S. Mayer, our commander, with the idea of doing a commemorative book about our battalion. I described it fully and explained why it was such a good idea. The book would be a tribute to our battalion, I explained—and it would certainly please the men (and the lieutenant colonel, I thought) to read about themselves and the time we had all spent together as a unit.

The book was to be the story of our basic training in the States, our landing in Cherbourg, our march across Germany, and our occupation duties in Austria. I wanted the book to be a tribute to the courage and heroic effort of our men.

When the colonel asked what I required to undertake and complete such a project, I said I needed a jeep, a travel pass, and the services of a beautiful Austrian Fräulein, who also happened to be a professional photographer. About a week later, the colonel agreed to the publication—with a parting shot. "Braziller, it better be good."

I quickly put together a team of three of my buddies. Joe Gibbs as editor, Stanley Spencer as managing editor, and Don Carnavalle in charge of photography. I was the publisher, in charge of making sure we had a finished book.

I ran into some luck. The army's Operational Publication division was stationed in Munich. It was responsible for publications of newspapers, posters, and pamphlets. The division was stationed in the building that formerly housed a Nazi newspaper, many of the things I needed were available to me.

So, working as a team, under pressure to complete the book quickly, with everyone's cooperation, we finished the book in fall 1945—with a salute to me from the colonel and a party to celebrate.

I hated to wear a helmet. Cherbourg, France, 1944

After the War

In the winter of 1945, along with tens of thousands of other boys, I was discharged from Camp Upton, the place where we had started. I felt pretty good, strutting around in my army uniform and air force parachute boots. My wife, Marsha, our little son, Jimmy, my mother, Rebecca, and one or two brothers and sisters met me at Penn Station. The welcome home party they threw for me was one for the books—an entire evening of nonstop crying, dancing, and singing.

When all the parties finally ended and things began to calm down, I went back to the office. After a two-and-a-half year absence, I was rather nervous about facing the more than 100 employees we now had, many of whom I didn't know. Marsha asked how I could be nervous about facing a few friendly employees after facing the Nazis. When we got off the elevator and walked into the office, there was no one in sight. I said we should look into the library. Empty. Then we entered the reception room.

I was greeted with a roar that sounded like the roar Babe Ruth heard when he hit another home run with bases loaded! I heard hurrahs and "Welcome home, George," over and over again. A trio of musicians was playing, and people were dancing and singing. They shouted, "Speech! Speech!" I was so taken aback with the emotion that swept over me that I almost began to cry. I choked out a few words of thanks to everyone for sticking by Marsha during my absence and for doing such a great job. Then I asked everyone to observe a minute of silence for the men and women who would *never* come home.

I found an apartment on West 70th Street in Manhattan, where Marsha, Jimmy, and I could live. I was eager to get back to work. When I left for the army, the Book Find Club had 20,000 members. Marsha had been running the club while I was away, and by the time I returned, the membership was at 50,000.

Logo designed by Cynthia Hollingworth, 1960

Part Three

Publishing

"In dreams begin responsibilities."
— William Butler Yeats

"The Memoir is a book of many parts, moving, stumbling toward a finished goal."—Oscar Wilde

Starting Out

Without knowing what it would cost financially or emotionally, I decided to start my own publishing house in 1955. On February 12, a bright, winter's day and my thirty-ninth birthday, George Braziller Publishers, Inc., hung out its shingle in cramped quarters on Madison Avenue at 33rd Street.

We couldn't afford the luxury of private offices, so all sat in small cubicles (the rage back then) and shouted to each other over the wall dividers. I had virtually no staff, but was fortunate to have George Brantl, a brilliant editor, and Herman Figatner, our treasurer. As always, Marsha was at my side, advising and encouraging.

I quickly learned to make proper contacts, to meet the people at the trade magazine *Publishers Weekly* and call on the editors of the *New York Times Book Review*. I had to be sure to meet the buyers at the many Doubleday bookshops, meet the book distributors, Baker and Taylor, and, most important, meet the buyer at the New York Public Library. Also to attend luncheons, arrange meetings with publishers and editors, buy drinks for people who could help me, and generally make my face familiar everywhere.

To my pleasant surprise, a call from Karl Kroch from Brentano's invited me to the weekly poker game, which was held at the Lotus Club on East 63rd Street in New York. Of course, I accepted and went one evening. There were half a dozen major figures in publishing at that game. I was very nervous meeting these big names in publishing: Cass Canfield, the head of Harper's Publishing; Lincoln Schuster, of Simon & Schuster; and Bennett Cerf, publisher of Random House. I also knew very little about poker. At one point during the game, Bennett Cerf said he had a joke to tell. Cerf was famous for telling jokes and for laughing before he finished telling his own joke. "There was this couple living in Scarsdale. They had to drive to Larchmont station to catch the morning train to New York. Just as they arrived at the station, the train started to pull away. The woman, very irritated, turned to the man and said, "You and your morning fuck."

After doing all the things a publisher would need to do, I made the next bold step. I went to Europe, where I felt that I might find new artists and writers—especially in Paris. I discovered the philosopher and playwright Jean-Paul Sartre, author of *The Words,* a brilliant account of his childhood. In 1964, Sartre won the Nobel Prize for Literature.

The novelist Claude Simon, another Nobel Prize winner and master of the experimental *nouveau roman,* also became one of the leading French writers on our list. In 1960, we published *The Flanders Road,* his terrifying account of the Battle of Verdun during World War I. Other French literary innovators I met included Nathalie Sarraute, Julien Gracq, André Malraux, and Claude Mauriac.

Through my professional friendships with these writers and during my frequent visits to Paris, I was led further, to discover new foreign writers: Carlo Emilio Gadda from Italy; Janet Frame from New Zealand; Scotland's Alasdair Gray, Kathleen Raine, and Beryl Bainbridge; Ireland's Neil Jordan, Desmond Hogan, and Brian McClaverty; and Orhan Pamuk from Turkey, also a Nobel Prize winner.

Well, dear reader, as you can see, I did what I had to do—which was, for me, the right thing to do.

Frankfurt

Fall is an exciting time of the year in the book publishing world. It comes after a long summer and after sales conferences and preparations for the Frankfurt Book Fair, the world's largest book fair, held each year. For five days, more than 280,000 visitors and more than 7,000 exhibitors from more than 100 countries take part. The event is considered crucial for making international book arrangements and meeting international publishers and authors. I found out quickly that it was almost as hard to get a hotel room in Frankfurt as it was to sign up a new writer.

I started going to the fair when I was just getting started in publishing in 1955. Frankfurt gave me the opportunity to meet famous publishers and authors from all over the world and to speak with them face-to-face. I am not touting Frankfurt or the other trade fairs, but if you work hard at them, they can be rewarding. For me, the biggest benefit was getting acquainted with some wonderful people and forming friendships that have lasted for many years. At Frankfurt, there are always select parties one hopes to be invited to or possibly crash. Getting an invitation to the annual Holtzbrinck Publishing Group luncheon means you have reached the ultimate.

That first year, I had a room in one of the most favored hotels in Frankfurt, the Hessicher Hof. The hotel wasn't favored only for its quality; the place was also very helpful in arranging meetings with publishers, editors, and authors. My days often started with brief breakfast meetings at 8 a.m.

The hotel dining room was filled with publishers from all over the world: among them, Collins from England, Gallimard from France, Einaudi from Italy. I nodded to some, shook hands with others. As I looked around the room and at the faces of various national groups, I suddenly thought of how proud I was to be in the profession of literary publishing. I got up from the breakfast table and headed for the fair in the company of another publisher or two. We discussed what we were doing and what we were looking for, what was new and exciting.

As I entered the fair, I headed for my display stand. The aisles were crowded. People were rushing to appointments. Some were late. Others were lost. I loved it.

Arriving at my stand, I sat down to catch my breath, set up my display of books, and happily waited, all the time shaking hands and waving at passersby and friends. I hoped to discover a new writer or sell one of our beautiful art books. I thought about which party to crash.

The first time I was in Frankfurt was during the cold winter of 1945, when I was still in uniform. The trains were not running at the Frankfurt international railway station. I was waiting for the U.S. Army trucks that would take me and my buddies to Hamburg and then to the United States. I had been away from home for almost two-and-a-half years. Looking out from the station, I was shocked by what I saw. The city was nothing but rubble as far as I could see—buildings flattened, street cars in shambles. There was no power or running water in many parts of the city, and only a few trucks crawled along the uprooted streets. I felt no pity for the Germans. I thought about Auschwitz, Belsen....

Now, it was 1955. I was back in Frankfurt at the same railway station. Looking out, I was again amazed by what I saw. Frankfurt was like a new city. The trains were running, new office buildings were up and functioning. The trolleys were running, the cars of current vintage, the people well dressed. It was astonishing to see, ten years later, the complete changes in the city, which was now hosting the world's largest international book fair.

That year, a number of publishers had been discussing the idea of boycotting the fair because of Germany's role in the Holocaust persecutions during World War II. I was among those publishers in favor of the boycott, but, because I realized how important the trip was to my business, I had finally decided to attend the fair—but I felt it was shameful of me to be there.

The Tale of Genji

I have often said one could start a publishing house simply by walking the halls of the Metropolitan Museum of Art on Fifth Avenue. If you don't get any ideas from what you see on the walls, go to the lectures. Meet the curators, who are always ready and willing to share their knowledge. If they don't have the answer, they will recommend the right person or department for you to call on.

One day, I attended a lecture at the Met by Professor Miyeko Murase, a curator at the museum. Naturally, I sat in on the lecture hoping to hear and learn something. Professor Murase's lecture was on *The Tale of Genji*, a "prose narrative" written by Murasaki Shikibu around A. D. 1000, considered one of the greatest masterpieces of not only Japanese literature but world literature.

After the lecture, I approached Professor Murase. I told her I enjoyed her lecture and the subject matter and quickly said I would be interested in discussing a publication. She looked surprised and quietly said, "I am sorry, I can't talk now. Why don't you call me at my office some time next week." I thanked her and said I would.

I called Professor Murase the following week. She told me that she had been thinking about a book on *The Tale of Genji*. If I were really interested, she said, she would mail me the outline. After reviewing her outline, I presented the highlights at our editorial meeting:

The Tale of Genji *is considered one of the world's literary masterpieces. It has provided inspiration for Japanese painters and is widely considered to be the first novel ever written. The story relates the amorous adventures of the shining prince. The book contains one of the most exquisite, complete, and beautifully preserved series of paintings that illustrate the tale.*

Murase's introduction examines each of the paintings in detail, describing the scene depicted, and summarizes in brief the key event from the tale. The fifty-four images illustrate one chapter each. Their small dimensions measure just over five inches square. These graceful paintings shimmer with beauty and delicacy.

There is something wonderful about my work as a publisher. I can start out the day with nothing but dreams and end up bringing something beautiful into the world.

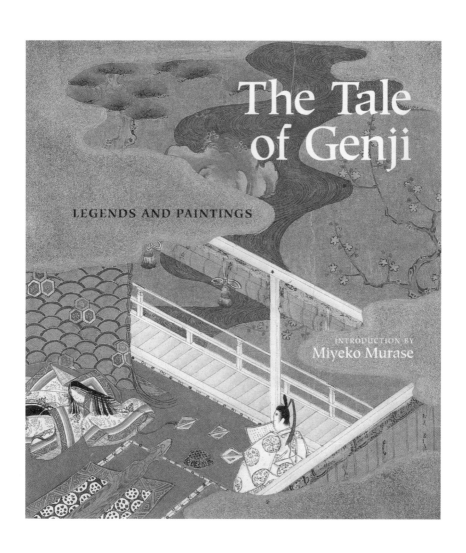

The Tale of Genji

LEGENDS AND PAINTINGS

INTRODUCTION BY
Miyeko Murase

THE GREAT AMERICAN ARTISTS SERIES

Ryder

Eakins

HOMER

de Kooning

Pollock

Davis

GEORGE BRAZILLER — PUBLISHER

American Artists

Creating the book series has long been a tradition with our publishing house. I found that series provided a way to explore the diversity of subject matter that interested me and, I hoped, would interest the book-buying public. Our series included everything from medieval manuscripts of the fourteenth and fifteenth centuries to the frescos of the great Italian artists and the masters of world architecture.

I had always wanted our publishing house to do something special on the subject of American art. So much of the art discussion during the 1950s and 1960s centered on the European painters, such as Dali, Matisse, Cezanne. I thought, why not retain a freelance editor with an American art history background and see what comes of it. After about a month of searching and asking around, we found the best person for the position: Tom Hess.

At the time, Hess was the editor-in-chief of *Art News* magazine. He had also written about many of the leading American artists, including Jackson Pollock and Willem de Kooning.

After many months of effort, we finally published a series of monographs called the Great American Artists Series. Within the series there was an equal representation of "traditional" artists and "modern" artists, with Albert Pinkham Ryder, Thomas Eakins and Winslow Homer in the former category, and William de Kooning, Stuart Davis, and Jackson Pollock in the latter. Each book contained a carefully chosen list of authors and illustrations—many in full color—that traced the development of and changes in each artist's work. I kept the price as low as possible to make the books available to a wide audience.

I did not undertake this series to counter the Parisian stranglehold on painting, but rarely had a new publishing venture received such extensive and unqualified praise from the critics. A full-page article by Aline Saasinen in the *New York Times* read: "Bravo for Braziller! For the first time American artists have been treated with a respect and faith heretofore reserved for their French counterparts."

Arthur Miller & Marilyn Monroe

I first met the playwright Arthur Miller in 1946, soon after my discharge from the army. My wife, Marsha, who had been running our Book Find Club, mentioned a first novel called *Focus,* written by a then relatively unknown writer, Arthur Miller. Marsha had found the book compelling and very timely and strongly urged me to read it, which I did. I agreed with her. The novel was about anti-Semitism in a small area of Queens on the border with Brooklyn.

We made *Focus* a Book Find Club selection and mailed out 40,000 copies to club members. The book brought the Miller and Braziller families together. We spent the summer of 1946 together in Mount Sinai, a small village on the north shore of central Long Island. Our families spent lots of time together in the following years.

With the release of his play *Death of a Salesman* in 1949, Arthur Miller won enduring fame. He talked to me about his newly won position in the literary world and how difficult it was for him to deal with the constant professional, financial, and political demands.

Senator Joseph McCarthy's anti-communist crusade was in full swing in the early 1950s. The House Un-American Activities Committee subpoenaed Arthur to answer questions. Arthur said the committee chairman, Francis Walter, offered to cancel the hearing if Walter could have his photograph taken with actress Marilyn Monroe, Arthur's soon-to-be wife. Arthur refused. He appeared before the committee and, to his credit, did not name names. To do so would have jeopardized the careers of many people. Arthur was found guilty of contempt of Congress, but the U.S. Court of Appeals overturned the conviction in 1958.

In the summer of 1947, Marsha (who was pregnant with our second son Michael) and I and our son, Jimmy, made our way to Martha's Vineyard, an island off the coast of Cape Cod, Massachusetts. We rented a small house in Vineyard Haven. It was not the "in" place to be, but it was beautiful, and my family loved it, even though we knew only a few people on the island. Well, we wised up eventually. The following summer we rented a yellow saltbox in Menemsha, which was also on Martha's

Vineyard. The house was small, but we had a great view of the harbor inlet. The next year, the house we rented gave us a little more room, so we were able to invite friends for weekends. We invited Arthur Miller, and the phone started ringing off the hook.

The buzz on the Vineyard was that Arthur Miller, the famous playwright, was on the island and staying at the Braziller house. The first few calls were, "Could Mr. Miller come for dinner?" "Well," I said, "Mr. Miller is my guest." Silence. "Well, all right, Mr. Braziller, you can come, too." When I told Arthur about the conversation he laughed. "What the hell," he said, "you will have a lot of free dinners while I am here."

In the late 1990s, I attended a performance of Arthur's play *The Ride Down Mt. Morgan.* I spotted Arthur in the audience and went over to him during intermission. We chatted briefly. On the following day, he invited me to lunch. I had the feeling he wanted to ask how I felt about the play.

During lunch, Arthur didn't start off the conversation by asking about the play. Instead, he asked how I was doing, what was happening in my publishing house, and a question or two about my personal life. Usually when I was with Arthur, he mainly talked about himself. During that luncheon I detected a change.

Nevertheless, I knew he wanted to talk about the play. I kept my comments brief. I stressed all the things I liked about it—the choreography, the staging, the characters, and the many scenes of real comedy. I could see he was expecting more, however. I cautiously led up to what I thought were some of its weaknesses. I simply said that I thought the ending could be strengthened, that it needed to pull together more effectively.

When we left the restaurant, I could see in his face the strain he was under. I was very touched by the regard he demonstrated that day for my opinion. Before we parted, he said, "What do you think, George? Do you think the play will work?" I didn't answer.

P.S.

Marilyn was beautiful—just gorgeous. She was always very demonstrative with Arthur, often draping her arm around him. He was quite shy and would pull away from her a little.

Marilyn loved dancing. Sometimes, when we were all together, we would put on a record. Marilyn often tried to pull Arthur onto the floor. He was shy and resisted, but eventually a smile would break out on his face and he would start dancing.

One night we were all together, having a great time. We were dancing and singing and it got to be quite late. Finally, we all went to bed. While in bed, I turned to Marsha and said, "Gee, I kissed Marilyn." "Big deal," she said. "Arthur kissed me."

The Question

In 1958, Charles de Gaulle had just formed the Fifth Republic of France. At the time, there was an uprising in the French territory of Algeria. Paris, the City of Lights, was paralyzed by a general strike led by supporters of Algerian independence.

Richard Seaver, my editor, walked into my office one afternoon. He was very excited about a recently published book that had been banned in France. This was the first time since the eighteenth century that France had banned a book on political grounds. The book was called *The Question,* written by Belgian journalist Henri Alleg.

From 1950 to 1955, Henri Alleg was the editor of the *Alger Républicain.* The newspaper was the only daily in Algeria that printed news about all aspects of Algerian democratic and national opinion. French authorities banned the newspaper in September 1955. In November 1956, Alleg went into hiding to escape internment. On June 12, 1957, during the Battle of Algiers, Alleg was arrested by French paratroopers, who held him captive for one month.

The Question is a graphic account of Alleg's detention in the El-Biar and Lodi torture chambers of Algiers. While at Lodi, he drew up a plea protesting the tortures he had endured. It was smuggled into France and received considerable publicity in the French and international press, exposing facts that the public had known nothing about until then.

After three days of negotiations with the French publisher, Editions de Minuit, Seaver obtained the rights to publish Alleg's book. Jean-Paul Sartre wrote the preface.

On June 16, 2013—fifty-six years after Alger's arrest, almost to the day—I read in the *New York Times* that President Obama has taken new steps in his effort to close down the U.S. military prison on Guantánamo Bay, Cuba. For many years, the prison has been notorious for its inhumane treatment of detainees. I regret to write that, as of October 2014, the prison is still open.

Michael Kruger on My 80th Birthday

On my eightieth birthday, I invited a number of friends and authors to a private dinner at the home of my dear and generous friends Sy and Victoria Newhouse. A few wrote back that they could not attend. Michael Kruger, author of two novels I published—*The End of the Novel* and *The Man in the Towers*—was more than gracious in his speech at my party. He caught the spirit of the bitter war years and our shared "belief in the continuity of the world."

Michael Kruger
Editor in Chief
Hanser Publishers
Munich, Germany

Dear George,

Everybody in this room knows that you are a great and devoted publisher. Everybody knows that you are a very individualistic publisher—one who is very much in love with his books, even those that fail to sell. Everybody in this room knows that you are fighting for a rare idea in publishing today—for beauty. So, I don't have to repeat the praise you will hear today for your work, which is embodied in the long row of books that you have published under your own name.

But I think I have to tell your friends here what you mean to me. You are—for me and forever in the annals of publishing—the first Munich publisher after the war. You showed me the book you printed in the offices of Oldenbourg Printers, right after coming to the city in May 1945, as an American soldier. You were twenty-nine years old at that time. It was the first uncensored book after thirteen years of brutal censorship in the "Hauptstadt der Bewegung."*

Today it is an icon of freedom and free press. You came to the destroyed city of Munich, you were put in the old Oldenbourg building, and what did you do? You printed a book, showing your comrades in photographs and telling their biographies. That's all. In my opinion, there is no better sign for belief in the continuity of the world—and of humanity—than to start in a destroyed house an old Heidelberg printing machine to produce a book of friendship. With your book, the war was over.

---

* During the Nazi regime, Munich was known as *Hauptstadt Der Bewegung,* Capital of the Movement.

The Hours of Catherine of Cleves

In the fall of 1964, *New York Times* art critic John Canaday wrote that the exhibition then at the Morgan Library "may prove to be the most dazzling art exhibition of the season." At the time, my office was just a short walk from the Morgan Library. I read Canaday's glowing review and decided to see the show on a lunch hour.

On the walls of the main exhibition room were more than 150 shadow boxes in which were displayed pages of the fifteenth-century manuscript *The Hours of Catherine of Cleves*. Every exquisite page captured my attention. A whole new world of art opened to me—the range of colors was dazzling and the details were astonishing, down to the tiniest leaves on the trees.

The Hours of Catherine of Cleves is considered the major work of an unknown Dutch master of miniature painting. Catherine commissioned it upon her marriage to the Duke of Guelders. The manuscript is a "book of hours," a type of devotional prayer book.

As usual, somewhat impulsively, I decided to publish this extraordinary work of art and devotion for the art-loving public. Fred Adams, the director of the Morgan, and I agreed to publish the work in facsimile as a joint venture. Two days later, I met John Plummer, the curator of the exhibition, who wrote the accompanying text in the facsimile edition. He described the twenty-year effort that went into the production of this great manuscript by a host of anonymous calligraphers, illuminators, and illustrators, resulting in this breathtaking work of art.

The planning was the easiest, and most pleasant, part of the project. Little did I realize the hard work that lay ahead of us. We had to find a printer who was familiar with facsimile reproduction and with mills that could supply paper that had the appearance of parchment. We needed four-color separation work that would include gold as a fifth color. Would it be possible to market a recently discovered fifteenth-century manuscript that was as unknown to the public as it was to me? Yet the successful publication of *The Hours of Catherine of Cleves* would pave the way for me to publish some of the most important medieval manuscripts in history during the next twenty years.

Anctissime ac beatissime
martir laurenti. sup
pliciter ego peccator ser
uus tuus pietatem tuam exoro
vt pro me spurcissimo multis
q; viciorum ponderib; oppresso
preces effundere digneris ad om
nipotentem deum quatinus

Janet Frame

Unsolicited manuscripts often arrived in our office, as they arrive in the offices of most publishers. They make the rounds of the editors, often receiving no more than a cursory glance before ending up in the "slush pile," the graveyard of forgotten manuscripts.

It was my practice on leaving the office to take a quick glance at our slush pile and perhaps take something home to read. I always hoped to find an unknown author who would take the publishing world by storm. Usually that sort of thing only happens in the movies. Still, I often worried that I might be, unawares, passing up a great opportunity.

In 1959, our fifth year of publishing, I picked up an unsolicited manuscript by Janet Frame, a writer born in New Zealand. It was actually a bound book, entitled *Owls Do Cry,* published by Pegasus Press in New Zealand. The book was a bit banged up, as though it had gone through a laundry cycle.

I looked at the flap copy and read: "This novel about a New Zealand family is by an author already distinguished for a book of brilliant short stories. The publishers believe that *Owls Do Cry* will prove an outstanding literary event." I'd heard that sort of promotional pitch before. I put the book down and didn't think much more about it. Just another local talent, I said to myself.

As I was leaving the office a few nights later, I noticed that someone had put the book in a box that contained papers and books we were planning to give away. I decided to take another look at it. I read the novel in one sitting. The flap copy was right. The book was one of the most original pieces of writing that I had read in a long time.

At the time, I was publishing the works of a group of French writers—Nathalie Sarraute, Jean-Paul Sartre, Claude Simon, and others—whom critics later termed the writers of the *nouveau roman* ("new novel"). These writers were pushing the boundaries of what we had long accepted to be the proper form for the novel. This new form was abstract, intangible, and yet completely authentic. As one critic claimed, it "sought the reality behind commonplace events."

Janet's form was less consciously new, but to me it was equally striking and powerful. Her writing reverberated not just through the abstract voices of the narrative, but through the variety of the experiences she depicted. As the flap copy described, she wrote in a poetic form that, "although grounded in recognizable experiences and memories, spoke ultimately to universal human concerns."

My professional relations with Janet extended for a period of more than thirty years. Our publishing house published her next eight novels, volumes of her poetry and short stories, and her masterful autobiography. I wished that our contact could have been closer, but New Zealand is a long way from New York. Neither one of us was a faithful letter writer, but I cherish the few letters I have from her. They reveal aspects of her that I might not have known had we actually been neighbors.

Usually, she wrote on different-colored papers. I was always on guard when letters on green paper arrived. Janet usually complained in her green letters, whereas the white and pink letters always carried friendlier thoughts.

As a young publisher, I was just beginning to understand what it meant to develop a list and to introduce new ideas to the public. I realized that there were no established guidelines regarding what to publish. I had to determine the guidelines for myself.

"Pretty Diane"

This sweet, wonderful poem arrived one day in my office, unsolicited. So typical of me, I rushed to open the mailbag, always hoping or expecting to find something extraordinary that might change my life. In the excitement, the envelope that the poem came in was lost, and the poet's name and address with it. I have saved this poem for more than thirty years, hoping someday to find the poet—or the pretty Diane.

I fell IN Love with a pretty DiaNe.

I fell IN Love with a pretty DiaNe
AND I did Not KNow
What I should done.

I will call her oN teLephoNe
to hear her voice again.
I would like this happiNess
For rest of my LiFe remain.

In this twentieth centure
Life is very hard,
to be with DiaNe is like adventure,
It is Like ▬▬▬ under the happy star.

Dear DiaNe, I miss You so much
I would Like to see You at once.
I will fly across the desert of sky aND space
To be in Your Peace.

Dear DiaNe, please correct my EngLish.
And iF this poem is not wrong
The composer will write a meLody
And this poem will become a song.

Meyer Schapiro

George always nurtured collaborative relationships with his editors. He gave us the freedom to propose ideas for books on many different subjects, and although we knew he wouldn't green-light every project, we felt confident that he would carefully consider each idea.

The highlight of my tenure as art editor was working with Professor Meyer Schapiro of Columbia University, the leading art historian of his generation. George had been publishing Schapiro's essays in volumes of selected papers since the 1970s to great acclaim. By the early 1990s, it was time for the fourth volume, Modern Art. *George asked me to usher the collection into print.*

For a period of several years, I would visit Meyer at his home, a veritable athenaeum on West 4th Street in New York. I would bring a set of modestly revised galleys, which he would slowly and carefully review. His lovely and accomplished wife, Lillian, was always present to oversee the process and gently prod his acceptance. Meyer was quite frail at the time, in his late eighties or early nineties.

Once the editorial discussions were over, Meyer would begin to talk about art: Romanesque sculptures that he had studied in France in the 1920s, insular manuscripts that he had examined in England, and artists whose studios he had visited in New York in the 1950s. He would become animated and seemed to transform into his younger self.

Over the course of my many meetings with Meyer and Lillian, I always knew that I was in the presence of two people of astonishingly rare qualities. One day, at their home, I found myself still surprised by the impassioned attraction that they felt for history, as well as the events going on around them. For having been a part of their lives, for having shared a friendship with both Lillian and Meyer Schapiro, I count myself as privileged.

—Adrienne Baxter Bell, former editor, George Braziller Publishers

The Interns

Publishing interns are mostly young women in their twenties who have arrived in New York looking for a job in publishing—*any* job. Some are willing to work for as little as ten dollars an hour; many are willing to work for nothing. They are usually looking for part-time work until their classes begin again in fall. Many say the same thing when asked why they want to get into publishing: "Oh, sir, I love books. I grew up on books."

Often, it seems, these young women live in Brooklyn, sharing a room with a friend or two. Their parents have set them up in a safe apartment and pay the rent for a trial period, with their daughter's promise to go back home if things don't work out within a specified time. Most of them do return home, sooner or later.

Over the years, even with full-time employees on my staff, I had always tried to make room for interns. If they were pretty, so much the better, but that wasn't a primary consideration—enthusiasm counted for a lot. There was something pleasant about coming into the office each morning and being greeted by fresh, smiling, and eager young faces after spending a grumpy evening alone. It got the workday off to a good start.

I have a confession to make. I have always wanted to be a teacher, to share my experiences with young people. Teaching gives me a feeling of accomplishment, and so I became a teacher to my interns, always willing to share my experiences in publishing and life with anyone who was willing to listen.

Tara Zapp, a nineteen-year-old intern, would often come into my office and ask questions about how I decided to sign on an author, how I chose to publish the books that interested me from among the many that crossed my desk. I always answered as well as I could, without sounding like I knew it all. Knowing it all is almost impossible in publishing. The biggest names in the business have made their mistakes, as I did. My mistakes were always made with the best intentions, however, so I am not ashamed of them.

One quiet, late Friday afternoon, Tara came to my office and asked to speak with me. She said she had just read a poem by Charles Simic, titled "Elementary Cosmogony," in the collection of his poems we had published. I was surprised and pleased and asked her why she particularly liked that poem. "Because it's you," she said. She left the poem with me, then turned and walked away. I read the poem, as I had done many times before, and broke down in tears.

Elementary Cosmogony

How to the invisible
I hired myself to learn
Whatever trade it might
Consent to teach me.

How the invisible
Came out for a walk
On a certain evening
Casting the shadow of a man.

How I followed behind
Dragging my body
Which is my toolbox,
Which is my music box,

For a long apprenticeship
That has as its last
And seventh rule:
The submission to chance.

— Charles Simic

Miró

I was first introduced to Joan Miró's art book, *Miro: A Toute Épreuve,* in the rare book division of the New York Public Library—a gold mine, where publishers, editors, and authors can pick up lots of book ideas. It was in the autumn of 1983, just a few months before Miró's death. The Swiss publisher Gerald Cramer originally published the artist's book in 1958 in a limited edition of 130 copies.

Art critic James Thrall Soby called it "one of the most triumphant feats of book illustration in our century." Indeed, this rare collaboration between Cramer, the Spanish artist Joan Miró, and the French poet Paul Eluard makes the book unique.

In the 1940s Miró began experimenting with the book form, illustrating works of poetry. He always gave his paintings poetic titles, which revealed themselves to the artist only through the gradual evolution of the work. The title and the visual imagery became one and the same. In *A Toute Épreuve* Miró's sensitivity to the word and the image reaches perfection.

Miró was absorbed by Eluard's poems, and Eluard was equally absorbed by Miró's forms. The two men were able to create a work in which, as critic Anne Hyde Greet perceptively noted in *Bibliophile,* "there is a complete interpenetration of text and image," to give an impression of "slipping from one medium to another . . . of crossing a frontier, from the world of mixed verbal and visual imagery, into the silent world of the image."

Gerald Cramer guided their collective efforts patiently throughout the eleven years it took to make the book. He brought to the project an essential understanding of the book form, which allowed for the fullest realization of the aims of both artist and poet.

The book was so important to Cramer it was difficult for him to give me permission to publish an edition, as if he were letting some valuable part of himself go. As I watched him struggle with his answer, I almost decided not to go forward. But I stood silently and waited and waited and finally he said yes.

JOAN MIRÓ

A TOUTE ÉPREUVE

Poems by Paul Eluard

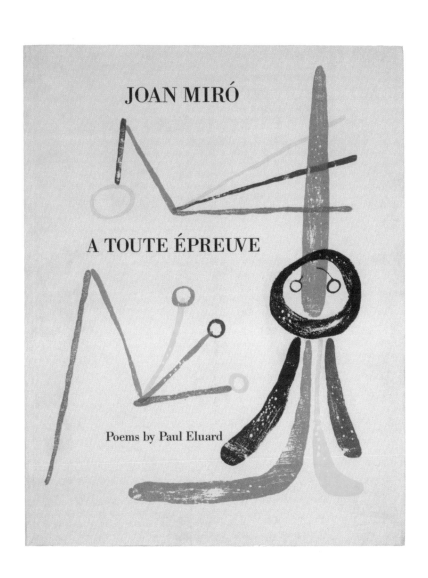

Nathalie Sarraute

I recall meeting the Russian-born French writer Nathalie Sarraute in Paris in 1962. We were introduced by Maria Jolas, the first translator of Sarraute's work into English. I was a new publisher and was looking for books representing what was new in writing. I had no idea at the time that she was one of the major pioneers of the *nouveau roman*.

Maria gave me her translation of Nathalie's *Portrait of a Man Unknown*. After reading it, I was baffled—and intrigued. This passage in Jean-Paul Sartre's introduction helped convince me to publish it:

> *The best thing about Nathalie Sarraute is her stumbling, groping style, with its honesty and numerous misgivings, a style that approaches the object with reverent precautions, withdraws from it suddenly out of a sort of modesty, or through timidity before its complexity, then, when all is said and done, suddenly presents us with the drooling monster, almost without having touched it, through the magic of an image.*

Naturally, I couldn't resist "the drooling monster." We eventually published nine of her books. Among my favorites are her novels *The Planetarium* and *Martereau* and her collection of essays, *The Age of Suspicion*.

Through the years, I enjoyed visiting Nathalie at her studio whenever I was in Paris.

I visited Maria, too, but I had to be careful about whom I visited first. When I called Maria to invite her to lunch, she'd say, "I suppose you've already called Nathalie." I would say, "No, no, I called *you* first." When I called Nathalie, she would say, "I suppose you've already called Maria." And of course I would say that I had called *her* first.

Nathalie was never particularly concerned about the critical reception of her books in America, but she did want to be sure that the English translations conveyed the tone and spirit of her work. "For Nathalie, a writer of poetic prose, it was the sound of the translation that mattered," explained Barbara Wright, another of Nathalie's translators. Sound was as important to her as meaning.

From the first day that I met Nathalie to our last meeting in Paris more than thirty years later, she never failed in her commitment to her writing. Her integrity, her devotion to her voice as a writer, motivated her throughout her life. When I last spoke to her months before she died, she was working on her next book.

As French literature scholar Ann Jefferson said in one review, Sarraute wrote of "the sensations, the impressions, the indefinable moments which flicker on the edges of consciousness in response to the almost imperceptible provocations that can come from the outside world in the form of a word, a gesture, a phrase, a tone of voice or accent, a hesitation or a silence."

Paris, February 1996

Dear George, how I regret not to be among your friends to say—or is it to sing?—"Happy birthday to you!"

It is quite long ago that we met for the first time. You were a young publisher and a very daring one, while you accepted Maria Jolas's proposal to publish my book, "Portrait of a Man Unknown," which she had translated.

It was refused everywhere in the States and you told me at that time that my first books were called "Braziller's Folly." But you went on being so reckless and never refused any of my books, in spite of the difficulty of finding readers for them.

Do you remember that when you came to Paris and I opened the door to you, I used to make the same joke: "O George, how could you afford it after my last one?" And you smiled and said: "Well, I have managed."

I want to express my gratitude for your confidence, your support. And also say that you are not only my publisher, but a very dear friend for whom I have a deep affection. So happy birthday, yes, with all my heart.

Nathalie

Richard Howard

Although I knew very little about contemporary poetry at the time I started my publishing house, for some reason I decided to add poetry to my program. I searched for someone who could help me shape such a list. I was extremely fortunate to have found such a person—Richard Howard, poet and translator, twenty-six years old.

What I liked about Richard was the fact that he was young and in close contact with his equally young contemporaries: Charles Simic, J. D. McClatchy, Carl Dennis, Rika Lesser. He had an open mind about modern poetry and played an important part in acquiring these poets for our publishing program. I knew Richard had good literary judgment, and he was invaluable to us as a reviewer and translator of French manuscripts. He translated about a half a dozen of our books.

Richard also helped our publishing house by being generous with his time and efforts. He often would forgo the standard fees for consultant and translator, to make possible the publication of an unknown poet. Among the poets we were proud to publish were Frank Bidart, Madeline DeFrees, Langston Hughes, Chester Kallman, David Malouf, Charles Simic, Rabindranath Tagore, and many others.

In 1970, Richard won a Pulitzer Prize for *Untitled Subjects*, a book of his poetry. Many of his translatations from French to English have been published and he has won several prizes for them, including a National Book Award for *Les Fleurs du Mal* by Baudelaire.

Ronald Glasser's *365 Days*

In 1967, America's war in Vietnam was still going on, and thousands, like me, who opposed the war were marching on the Pentagon to end the cruel and senseless fighting and bring the troops home. Among those who supported the war were the writers John Updike and John Steinbeck. I was very disappointed to learn of their position, as I had long admired both writers. When American involvement ended six years later, 45,933 American service men and -women had been killed, and 303,000 wounded.

One day, in 1969, I received a call from my dear friend, the art historian Dore Ashton. She told me about a friend, Ronald Glasser, a doctor who had served in Vietnam. She was reading his manuscript, *365 Days,* and asked if I would meet the doctor. I said of course I would. Glasser showed up at my office so quickly, it seemed as though he had been sitting in the waiting room.

Here he was, a young doctor recently returned from military service, holding his manuscript, hoping to see it published, asking if I would read it. I was taken at once by his boyish appearance—I believe he was in his late twenties, early thirties at the time. He spoke of the role he had played in the burn ward of a U.S. Army hospital at Camp Zama in Japan. It was so painful to hear his story, I had to interrupt him and ask him to leave the manuscript with me. I invited him to return the next day.

I read the manuscript, struck by his moving account of men in battle and the horrors of what he experienced in the burn unit. Many of the injured were soldiers who had been shot down and trapped in their burning helicopters. I could only think of that Christmas Eve in 1944, when a German submarine torpedoed an American troop ship positioned nearby in the English Channel. My buddies and I rushed to the horrible scene at the hospital to give blood and help the hundreds of wounded. Every Christmas Eve, I think about that one.

The next day, Glasser was waiting for me in the lobby. I shook his hand and said, "Ron, you have written one helluva goddamn good book, and we're going to publish it." After forty years and fifteen printings, *365 Days* is still in print.

Ronald Glasser

Ned Rorem

Interviewer: Louis Sheaffer
Place: Offices of George Braziller, Inc.
Date: September 16, 1980

Sheaffer: You have published a number of books by Ned Rorem, a leading American musical composer, starting with *The Paris Diary* in 1966. How did you happen to do this? How did he happen to come to you?

Braziller: At that time Robert Phelps, who was working here as an editor, was a good friend of Ned Rorem. Rorem was completely unknown to me because, while I had vaguely heard about him as a composer, he had been living in Paris for many years before he returned to America about 1966. My memory of that was that one day musical sheets. . .

Sheaffer: Is that the name of something—"Musical Sheets"?

Braziller: Well, no, they would be sheets that a composer would use to compose and make musical notes. Bob Phelps said it ran close to three-quarters of a million words.

Sheaffer: Oh, the manuscript was on musical sheets?

Braziller: Yes, he had written on them. It was amazing that Rorem—a young man in his thirties—could see fit to write a kind of diary of between half a million to three-quarters of a million words all on musical sheets. We were all panicked by the idea, but, at any rate, I asked Bob to let me look at it and, glancing at it before we made a decision, I found that there was sufficient interest in the manuscript for me to suggest that we might be interested in publishing it, provided that Rorem would agree to considerable editing.

Rorem took back the manuscript and agreed to look at it again, and we did cut considerably—or edit, which is a nicer word than cutting—and got it down to really the essence of what would make for an interesting diary. Subsequently we published it, and it was very well received by the critics. It had a freshness to it.

Sheaffer: Not only a freshness, but fresh in terms of insolence, I should say.

Braziller: It was an insight into the world of music and the Paris world. He was a student, I believe, of [French composer and conductor] Nadia Boulanger, whom he worshipped, and, of course, he knew Stravinsky and the whole world of music in Paris. The *Diary* deals with a great deal of that world.

Sheaffer: High-class gossip.

Braziller: High-class gossip, and that's what maybe the public wanted—lots of names, lots of incidents. Rorem wanted to do everything for posterity. He had a strange attitude about himself and about life. He really wanted to be immortal and he truly… I am certain that one of the reasons that he goes on writing is that he feels that the books will remain long, long, long after he is gone. He indicated as much to me. He has a certain obsession with death. Well, perhaps we all do, but it was surprising that a man as young as Rorem at the time talked about death the way he did, a man who is charming, very kind, and at the same time terribly vain, terribly vain. He would call periodically. Now, you said a moment ago about gossip, and here I am gossiping myself.

Sheaffer: Oh no, this is character description, really. This is not gossip, no, absolutely not.

Braziller: Good, because I am very fond of Ned Rorem and I have respect for him. I don't know how good a composer he is—that's for others to decide.

The Brooklyn Book Festival Award

In the spring of 2012, when I was first told that I would receive the Brooklyn Book Festival's award—given to a book publisher for the first time—I was going to refuse it. I am the nervous type, especially when I have to give a speech, but my friends convinced me to accept.

Weeks before the award ceremony, I practiced reading my speech over and over, while looking in the mirror. Two days before the event, Carolyn Greer, the executive director, called to say there had been a change of plans. There would be no speeches.

Here is the speech that I never made:

Thank you, Brooklyn Borough President Marty Markowitz, and thank you, Carolyn Greer, Executive Director, for the Brooklyn Book Festival's Book Mark award. Thanks also to my staff, who helped make it possible for me to be here tonight, and to the many authors who helped shape our publishing house.

It is often said that half of the people in publishing worked for my house at one time or another. It is also true that the other half did not want to work for it. To all of you, thank you. Much love.

I am often asked what one thing was most important in my sixty-year-long career in book publishing. I can only answer by saying there is no one thing.

The second most important thing is how grateful I am for the knowledge I have gained during those years—and for the loyalty of my staff and colleagues.

I am not sure if there is a third thing—but if there is, I will find it

Unsolicited Manuscripts

Most publishing houses receive hundreds of unsolicited manuscripts for consideration every year, but they rarely open the packages to examine the contents. The expense of dealing with such a high volume of material is prohibitive, not to mention the sheer waste, in most cases, of valuable office time and editorial patience, which are usually limited under the best circumstances. A more important consideration is the possibility of being accused of stealing someone's idea.

As a result, most unsolicited packages remain unopened and are dumped into what is called a slush pile, with the post office's cancellation date still visible on the stamps. Publishers will, however, most likely open and give due consideration to submissions from literary agents. The fate of an aspiring author often rests on being able to get an agent to take him or her on as a client.

Because agents considered our author advances small and felt we did not advertise on a large enough scale, Braziller Publishers rarely received submissions from agents, except for a few whose judgment we relied on. We *did* look at those unsolicited submissions, but we rarely found unsolicited material suitable for publication.

Twenty percent of our books came from agents and other sources. Nearly eighty percent of our publications grew out of suggestions from our own editorial staff—George Brantl, Richard Seaver, Adrienne Baxter. It was an exciting challenge to sit in our weekly editorial meetings, discussing the latest publishing gossip—what was selling, the new Nobel Prize winners—and kicking around ideas for possible publication.

Great Drawings of the Louvre Museum

One of my many great pleasures is the complexity of publishing illustrated art books, and an opportunity to do so presented itself with the series Great Drawings of the Louvre Museum. In this three-volume set of Italian, French and German, Flemish and Dutch drawings, magnificent works of art represent every school of great draftsmanship.

After signing a contract with the Louvre, I spent lots of time in the museum's Cabinet des Dessins, which contains one of the world's most magnificent collections of drawings. Curators Roseline Bacou and Maurice Sérullaz wrote the introductions and text for each of the books. I spent several days with these dedicated art historians in the archives.

When I arrived at the Louvre, I would climb the stairs to the fourth floor of the museum. The ascent was my morning workout, which ended in the most magnificent surroundings imaginable.

What an experience! Drawing after drawing, safely stored in archival cases, was laid before me on a great oak table. I was able to hold in my own white-gloved hands the very sheets of paper that had been held by the hands of Michelangelo, Cranach, Rubens, and Dürer. I was well aware that the opportunity to hold these drawings was a privilege granted to few. It was a very humbling experience. I remember viewing with great emotion the portraits by Holbein the Elder and Younger, the Grünewalds, and Rubens.

The artists had worked with every type of material: pencil, chalk, pen-and-ink, brush, watercolor and pastel. Traces of their fingerprints and erasures were still visible. Their personalities were evident in every mark they made. So we made our choices for the book, selecting from hundreds of these masterpieces—a difficult, almost impossible challenge, but we loved it. The success of each volume was due to the meticulous accuracy of the editor, Victoria deRamel. Victoria also provided the translations.

To this day, those hours in the Louvre remain among the most exciting experiences of my career. They were also invaluable in learning how to collaborate on a project as a member of a team.

Every day, before leaving the museum, I would stop for a while to look again at Leonardo da Vinci's masterpiece, the *Mona Lisa*.

Etching by Rembrandt

Orhan Pamuk

While I was in London on one of many scouting trips, I met with Cannongate Publishers. They mentioned a book they were about to publish—*White Castle* by Orhan Pamuk, a new, young Turkish writer. They said that a number of American publishers had already shown interest in the book, and if I were interested, I would have to decide quickly.

While reading the manuscript, I recognized how good Victoria Holbrook's translation was and, most important, what a fine storyteller Pamuk is. The novel was entertaining and witty. From the beginning, I was drawn into the story of the young Italian scholar and his double. I also loved reading about the conflicts and contradictions of Eastern and Western culture. Halfway through the book, I knew I would make every effort to acquire the rights.

Back at the office, my brilliant editor, Mary Taveras, gave the manuscript a second reading and confirmed my opinion. We called Cannongate and made an offer—which was accepted, to our great joy. What a good feeling it was to be able to acquire the first book of a writer I admire so much and to introduce him to an American audience.

The privilege of publishing Orhan Pamuk, who later won the Nobel Prize, does a great deal for a publishing house, especially when you are a small, independent house like Braziller. Publishing great writers gets the attention of other writers and literary agents, who are then motivated to submit manuscripts to your house. You do what you can to hold onto him or her. You prepare interviews, advertise (if you can afford it), and try to make the author happy. Most publishers, however, face problems trying to hold on to their best-selling authors. The fear of losing them is always present, as was the case for me with Pamuk.

One day the New York publisher Roger Straus called me to say that Pamuk's latest book was being offered to other publishers, including Straus. I told Roger I would regret losing Pamuk, but if I did, I hoped Roger's house would get him. I was very touched by Roger's call (he was the only publisher who called me) and was glad that he ultimately did acquire and publish Pamuk's second book.

The White Castle

A Novel by

Orhan Pamuk

Alessandra Comini

Yes, it did seem a breeze, or rather more of a whirlwind, to me, publishing three books with the legendary George Braziller of New York. Our first meeting, right after a lecture I'd given on the Viennese Expressionist artist Egon Schiele at the Guggenheim Museum in the fall of 1965, was magical. Standing silently by the speaker's podium, patiently waiting his turn to speak with me, was an intelligent-looking man with energetic face and merry, penetrating eyes. "Miss Comini..." he began. "Ms.," I corrected him. "Ms. Comini, I'd like to talk to you about writing a book on Gustav Klimt."

"What about Schiele?" I asked vehemently, still intent on the compelling artist with whom the lecture had been engaged, and not yet realizing he was a publisher. "That's possible too," was his swift answer in a deep voice that resonated with warmth and droll humor. Appreciative of my Italian name, he issued an invitation to meet the next day at an Italian bar and restaurant on West 39th Street, and I accepted. What was to have been an hour's lunch spun into a three-hour joust with serious talk squeezed in between ready repartee concerning art and the art world.

The very next year George came through with his latent promise to do a companion volume on Schiele. This time he allowed himself to be persuaded to include a "photograph album" of some fifty-plus rare images of Schiele, along with forty-eight color plates and sixty-one black-and-white text illustrations.

At my next lecture in New York at the Neue Galerie, George not only appeared, he had a bouquet of flowers sent to my hotel room. That bouquet sums up George Braziller for me: always blooming, always colorful, always full of new buds, new ideas, new projects, and new enthusiasms.

— Alessandra Comini, Distinguished Professor of Art History Emerita at Southern Methodist University

Signing the contract

Let America Be America Again

I met Antonio Frasconi in the 1950s when visting him at his studio in Washington Square in lower Manhattan. I commissioned him to create woodcut illustrations for a few of our dust jackets. Frasconi later became well known for his portraits of great artists and writers who inspired his art and his life. He illustrated many books and published hundreds of prints and folios. He also took great pride in his teaching and in the many hundreds of students who studied with him.

When I later visited Frasconi at his country home in Norwalk, Connecticut, he was in his nineties. He was slightly hunched, perhaps from so many years of bending over his wood blocks. He had a singsong quality to his voice when he spoke. He thrived on reminiscing and loved gossip, and I enjoyed listening to him. "Oh, George," he would say in that singsong voice of his.

While browsing through his studio during that visit, a book with a colorful cover and title grabbed my attention: *Let America Be America Again.* World-renowned poet and master of prose Langston Hughes enlightened Americans nationwide when his poem "Let America Be America Again" appeared in 1936. In celebration of the poem's inspiring message, Frasconi had illustrated the poem with thirty-two color woodcuts, adding a rich visual dimension to the poet's inspiring verses. Each pairing of stanza and image conveys the artist's dream of justice for all with compelling force.

I suggested to Antonio that we bring out a facsimile edition of the illustrated poem to reach a wider public. He hesitated at first, but I called him about a week later and asked about the project again. I was greatly pleased and gratified to hear him say, "Yes, you have my permission." It is astonishing that, almost eighty years later, this poem's insights into American society and its dream of social justice continue to resonate powerfully among readers.

O, YES,
I SAY IT PLAIN.
AMERICA NEVER WAS AMERICA TO ME,
AND YET I SWEAR THIS OATH –
AMERICA WILL BE!
AN EVER-LIVING SEED,
ITS DREAM

LIES DEEP IN THE HEART OF ME.

WE, THE PEOPLE, MUST REDEEM
OUR LAND, THE MINES, THE PLANTS,
                    THE RIVERS,

THE MOUNTAINS AND THE ENDLESS
                    PLAIN —
ALL, ALL THE STRETCH OF THESE
                    GREAT GREEN STATES
AND MAKE AMERICA AGAIN!

Langston Hughes

EINSTEIN'S
1912 MANUSCRIPT
ON THE
SPECIAL THEORY
OF RELATIVITY

Albert Einstein

The time was right for celebration. The world was entering a new century, and my publishing house was bringing out a book we hoped would be the book of the century: *Einstein's 1912 Manuscript on the Special Theory of Relativity.*

The volume displays Albert Einstein's own handwriting on the right-hand pages, with an exact translation of the text on the facing left-hand pages. Those with the ability to do so are able to make a line-for-line comparison. The original size of the manuscript pages forbids much reduction, so the pages are reproduced at actual size in facsimile, in order to avoid doing Einstein and the reader a disservice.

Einstein's "Special Theory of Relativity" is one of the most influential documents of the twentieth century—or, for that matter, any century. The manuscript shows extensive reworking, revealing Einstein's thought processes.

In the introductory text, physicist Peter G. Bergmann, a colleague of Einstein's, wrote: "Einstein's hand-written manuscript, with its corrections and emendations, is today a treasure, which enables us to observe and to follow to some extent the mental processes of one of the great minds of mankind."

During the book's production, I found it hard to contain my excitement at the privilege of being able to hold in my hands each of the seventy-two handwritten pages of Albert Einstein's transcendentally great manuscript. It was at such moments that I felt my life in publishing had been worthwhile. The project would not have been possible without the help of the late Philip Grushkin, a great American book designer, calligrapher, and human being.

We didn't know it at the time, while we were doing all this celebrating about the Einstein book, but we were about to experience a major loss. We simply let the book's success go to our heads. We launched our first advertising campaign, hired two new staff members, rented a larger office, and increased the quantity of books in the print run—all of which was damn expensive. Suddenly, the book stopped selling. We started getting returns of unsold copies from bookstores. It took us six months to pay off our debt. So much for success.

Will Barnet

One of the magical aspects of publishing is the serendipitous way by which books are created. I learned this important lesson while working on The World in a Frame. *The book brought together two strands of George Braziller's publishing program—literature and art—and was created on the heels of several books that Braziller had published in the mid-1980s.*

The year 1986 marked the centenary of Emily Dickinson's death. To mark the occasion, Braziller published a short introduction to her poetry, Emily Dickinson: Lives of a Poet *by Christopher Benfey—then an up-and-coming and now a formidable and well-established scholar. Benfey's book offered an overview of Dickinson's life, a well-crafted synthesis of the main themes in her poetry, and a thoughtful selection of her most well-known and loved verses.*

Soon after the Dickinson volume was published, I visited Will Barnet, a well-known American artist, in his studio in the National Arts Club building in New York. While looking at his paintings, I noted that his work evoked nineteenth-century New England, which was not surprising in that Will had grown up in Massachusetts. Will, in turn, mentioned that he loved the poetry of Emily Dickinson and would like to have a copy of the Benfey book. The next day, I sent him a copy. A few weeks later, he called to let me know that he had created a series of drawings inspired by Dickinson's poetry. Back to his studio I went to look at the drawings. They were extraordinary.

Each visualized and eerily captured the tone and emotions that Dickinson had so eloquently conveyed in word and sound. The work was truly a marriage of word and image. Once he saw the drawings, Braziller instantly comprehended the uncanny affinity between Barnet's images and Dickinson's poetry. George invited Will to do a series of drawings that would be published with the poetry that had inspired them. Benfey was commissioned to write an introduction to the work. And so, an artist's book was born.

I have wonderful memories of each of the projects upon which I worked during my years at Braziller. This book, though, has a special place in my heart. I was witness to the creative process and the synergy that took place

between a gifted artist, great poet, and a creative publisher. I learned about the importance of chance in the publishing process—and I was reminded of the power of the book, that technological wonder of consecutively turned pages that serves as a platform in which the whole is greater than the sum of parts.

—Beatrice Rehl, former Art History Editor for George Braziller Publishers

Australia

In February 1989, while on a scouting trip in Australia and New Zealand, looking for new authors, I took the opportunity to visit and revisit a few of our house's longtime Australian authors: Gail Jones, David Malouf, and Keri Hulme. I kept in touch with the office, as I was concerned about the Salman Rushdie affair. Recently, I was amused to come across the following fax to my staff in New York:

> *Dear Staff,*
>   *Tired but invigorated. Wellington and Sydney are two of the most beautiful harbor cities in the world. I am reading a novel by the Italian writer [Leonardo] Sciascia:* Candido or A Dream Dreamed in Sicily. *There is a passage in which the character Candido has a fantastic image of two people enwrapped and hidden by funereal climbing vines. I could not help thinking of the wrappings of Christo and how great it will be when he wraps the Reichstag in Berlin. He could wrap it with funereal climbing vines to show what this monstrous building stood for. Please fax a clean copy of the fax statement that came from Iran in which Islamic extremists reiterate the* fatwa *on Rushdie.*
>   *Regards,*
>   *Braziller*

Salman Rushdie

In 1993, I read about a book recently published in France entitled *Pour Rushdie*. It contained 100 essays by Arab and Muslim writers, expressing their support for Salman Rushdie's novel *The Satanic Verses*. Iran's religious leader, the Ayatolah Khomeini, considered the novel a blasphemy against the religion of Islam. He had issued a *fatwa* on the author's life in 1989. The writers who contributed to *Pour Rushdie* were proclaiming their support for freedom of expression as a universal right.

I had long admired Rushdie after reading his book *Midnight's Children*. I discussed the new book with my editor, Mary Taveras, and decided to obtain the rights to publish it in America. I called Editions La Découverte, the French publisher in Paris, and obtained the rights over the phone. Projects of this sort really get me going.

In an extraordinary collective act of courage, 127 Iranians risked their lives and safety to sign a statement of support for Rushdie, which is also included in the book. Opposition to injustice often brings about personal suffering: The Italian translator of the *Satanic Verses* was seriously wounded, and the Japanese translator was killed. Rushdie lived underground for almost ten years with the *fatwa* hanging over him. Iran's president lifted the death threat in 1998, but the *fatwa* was reissued in 2012, blaming Rushdie for an anti-Islam film with which he was not affiliated.

As the American publisher of *For Rushdie,* we received phone threats at home and at the office. It was necessary to change our phone numbers a few times, and we engaged a security guard at the office for a brief period.

Samuel Menashe

Samuel Menashe, a New York poet of short verse, died in 2011 at the age of eighty-five. As I read the obituary in the *New York Times,* I learned that he had participated in the Battle of the Bulge in World War II. Out of his unit of 300 men, there were only 20 survivors. It was typical of this self-effacing man that he never mentioned this experience when I first met him—or even when I got to know him better.

In 1971, *No Jerusalem But This,* Menashe's collection of poems on Jewish themes, was published in the United States. His work had already received praise and attention in Britain. It was not until 2004, when Menashe received the first Neglected Masters Award from the American Poetry Foundation, that America really recognized his work.

I first met Samuel when he visited my office. I knew very little of his background and had a limited idea of his work as a poet. During our conversation, I asked the usual questions publishers ask authors: Why did you write this poem? When did you finish your latest work? What are you planning next? and so forth.

Menashe politely indulged my questions. I told him how difficult it was to sell poetry to the general public. Everyone in publishing knows that only poets, for the most part, buy poetry—and there are not enough of them to support the cost of publication. Menashe sat there, listening, confident, with a knowing smile. He agreed in a gracious manner that it was indeed difficult to sell poetry. He said he completely understood the problem and sympathized with my situation, given the current state of publishing. Before he left my office, however, I asked him to leave his manuscript with me. I promised to read it and to give it my full attention. Reluctantly, I ultimately rejected it for publication.

On one occasion, I met Menashe in Central Park. He had invited me to attend one of his readings of Shakespeare's sonnets, which he read before a select group at the statue of the Bard in the park's Shakespeare Garden. I attended his reading—which was eloquent, enlightening, and rich in sound. When I left the garden, I walked down the long esplanade of tall trees toward the exit on Fifth Avenue, thinking how fortunate I was to know a man like Menashe.

These days, when I'm in the park, I sometimes see him coming toward me—slight of build, hair a sandy color, navy blue shirt open at the collar, a paperback under his arm. He sees me, smiles, skips a step, and extends his hand for a handshake, with a warm, "Hello Braziller, what brings you to the park?" "My companions," I replied. "The trees."

THES DAYS WHEN I'M IN THE PARK, I SOMETIMES
SEE HIM COMING TOWARDS ME - SLIGHT OF
BUILD, HAIR A SANDY COLOR, NAVY BLUE SHIRT
OPEN AT THE COLLAR, A PAPERBACK UNDER HIS
ARM, HE SEES ME, SMILES, SKIPS A STEP, AND
EXTENDS HIS HAND FOR A HANDSHAKE. WITH A
WARM, HELLO BRAZILLER, WHAT BRINGS
YOU TO THE PARK? "MY COMPANIONS.
THE TREES."

Fresco Cycles of the Renaissance

When in Florence in the spring of 1991, I visited the Brancacci Chapel in the Church of Santa Maria del Carmine to see the Renaissance painter Masaccio's great mural. I paid a few *lire* to the old caretaker of the chapel, who then politely turned on the lights so I could see the fresco in all its glory.

During that same visit to Florence, I walked up the long hill to Villa I Tatti. The villa is the world's foremost research institute for Italian Renaissance arts and also the home of renowned Renaissance historian Bernard Berenson. The art historian Millard Meiss, professor at Princeton University, was in residence there for the season. In 1968, Meiss had arranged a monumental exhibition at the Metropolitan Museum of Art entitled *The Great Age of Fresco: Giotto to Pontormo,* which had a great impact on me. Meiss had invited me to visit him at the villa, and I spent that afternoon touring the beautiful home and grounds of the estate. At one point, Meiss asked if I would like to sit in Berenson's chair in his study. The view from the windows was breathtaking, with the entire city of Florence visible through the cypresses that flooded the view.

Later I rented a car in Florence and drove along the twisting highway, taking in the glorious vista, on my way to Siena, where I would spend the day in the Palazzo Pubblico, home to the spectacular frescoes by the Sienese painter Ambrogio Lorenzetti. There I viewed Lorenzetti's *Allegory of Good Government,* painted in 1340, the very first secular fresco cycle since antiquity.

I subsequently published *Ambrogio Lorenzetti: The Palazzo Pubblico, Siena* by Renaissance historian Randolph Starn along with nine other volumes.

With the success of Meiss's book on the Metropolitan's exhibition, my art editor, Adrienne Baxter, was able to approach other noted scholars to write about the frescoes in which they were interested. Nine art historians, each a specialist in his or her own field, graciously accepted the proposal. I marveled at what these authors and Adrienne were able to accomplish. The frescoes the authors selected together represented some of the greatest achievements in Renaissance art.

Ambrogio Lorenzetti

The Palazzo Pubblico, Siena

From Haven to Home

From an early age, I knew only a little about Jewish life in America. I grew up in a neighborhood in which there were many Jews. Through my aunts and uncles, I managed to pick up some of the highlights of Jewish life. I learned about Rosh Hashanah, Yom Kippur, and Passover. I loved the rituals and traditions that went with these holy days. On Yom Kippur, if you beat your breast with your fists, you are freed of all the sins you committed during the past year—I got away with an awful lot this way.

The holy days were also occasions for dressing up in your best clothes. How excited I was watching my mother and sisters getting dressed! How proud I was when we walked, as a family, along Sutter Avenue—my mother leading, I and my two sisters trailing behind—to the nearby *shul,* which was nothing but a poor storefront on Hendrix Street.

When older, as I assumed marital and family responsibilities, I felt inclined to broaden my interests—professionally, socially and politically. I received a call from Michael Grunberger, who was then head of the Hebrew section at the Library of Congress, asking if my publishing house might be interested in producing a book on a forthcoming exhibition about Jewish life in America. What I had been searching for had simply dropped in my lap, something that doesn't happen very often in publishing.

I made the trip to Washington, D.C., to discuss the project with Grunberger. The early phase of the publishing process is always exciting. I love to participate in and observe the making of a new book. I enjoy the give-and-take between publisher, author, and editor, about the necessary details of book size and paper, illustrations, and so forth. Above all, I love the feeling that I might contribute to and learn something new about a subject in which I am developing a new interest. The book would be titled *From Haven to Home: 350 Years of Jewish Life in America.*

Grunberger handed me a brief outline of what the book would contain, a table of contents, and a list of eminent Judaic scholars. The book would include a chapter about the first Jewish group to arrive in New Amsterdam in 1654 and establish the first synagogue in North America.

The book would also include chapters on the Jewish contributions to American culture and life through the present day. It would address the role of Jewish soldiers in the Civil War and the two world wars and would portray the struggles of American Jewish men and women in U.S. politics. The book would also mention the first Bible printed in the United States and the subsequent printing of Jewish literature and Torahs. It would be a story of America and American ideals.

Acquiring this important book was not just a bit of good fortune for my publishing house, it was a bit of personal luck as well. Not only did it celebrate 350 years of Jewish life in America, its publication in 2004 was one year before my own celebration of 50 years in book publishing.

George at the age of fifteen supporting a strike.

George Braziller outside the New York Public Library, protesting the invasions of Irag and Afghanistan.

Afghanistan

On May 19, 2010, the *New York Times* ran photos of the faces of 1,000 American soldiers who had been killed in Afghanistan since the Bush administration invaded that country in 2001, in response to the terrorist attacks of September 11, 2001. I spread the paper across my office desk and started counting—hundreds of these soldiers were less than twenty-three years of age. I was so upset I broke down in tears. I said to my editor and colleague, Maxwell Heller, "We've got to do something about this."

I put together a signboard and mounted the pages from the *Times*. While Maxwell managed the office, I went down to the Battery in Lower Manhattan and stood in the park with the sign around my neck. I knew that most of the people who were boarding the ferry there were tourists heading for the Statue of Liberty. I wanted them to know what was going on in our nation. From there, I headed to the New York Public Library and stood alone on the steps, wearing the sign, as crowds of New Yorkers walked past me, curious about what I was doing.

At the time of writing, the illegal war in Afghanistan continues. The U.S. Defense Department estimates that 2,317 American service members have died in Afghanistan in the twelve years since the American invasion.

Marc Chagall

Longus's ancient Greek story of Daphnis and Chloe, who were destined to fall in love, inspired the artist Marc Chagall to create a book. He visited Greece twice to capture the lyrical effects and color of the light, which he brought to his 1961 edition of the tale. Chagall not only gave the myth a new intimacy, he made it a modern romance.

I went to Paris and called on the French publisher Tériade to ask for permission to publish *Daphnis and Chloe* in the United States. His permission was not difficult to get—he was pleased with what I had accomplished with our edition of Matisse's *Jazz*—but he said that Chagall would also have to grant permission.

I made an appointment with Chagall and called on him at his Paris apartment. When I knocked on the door, Chagall himself opened it. He greeted me with a big smile and a *bonjour.*

He walked me to a big table in his studio, which was cluttered with brushes, books, loose prints and magazines, and tubes and bottles of paint. He was wearing a red-checkered shirt, and his grey hair was brushed back. His full face was unlined. He looked at me with his bright eyes and said, "I know why you are here, but I don't know who you are or why you want to publish *Daphnis and Chloe.*"

I told him that I had admired his work for many years. In 1967, we had published a book of his famous work in stained glass, The Jerusalem Windows, although I had not met Chagall at that time. After seeing his illustrations for *Daphnis and Chloe,* I knew I wanted to introduce the book to a wider audience, especially to an American audience, which was unacquainted with such fine editions. I explained that I needed his permission to proceed with the project.

Chagall began to ask me questions about poets. He read a lot of poetry, he said, and wrote poetry himself. I told him that I had published Nobel Prize winners Jean-Paul Sartre and Claude Simon. But when I mentioned the Caribbean poet Aimeé Césaire, his face lit up and he cried, "Bravo!"

Chagall spoke English quite well. He had lived for a time on

New York's Lower East Side. While there, he walked through the neighborhood, seeking the Jewish foods, the people, and the sounds of the Yiddish language in order to feel at home.

After an hour or two, as Chagall walked me to the door, I realized I wasn't sure I had gotten what I had come for. Suddenly he took my arm, looked at me, and said, "You have my permission."

When the door closed behind me, I waited a few minutes. As I descended the stairs, I thought to myself, "Boy, am I glad that's over." I didn't realize how nervous I had been.

Anselm Kiefer

I first learned of the German artist Anselm Kiefer when Anthony D'Offay, a British art dealer and Kiefer's gallery agent, visited my office. Kiefer was then one of the most acclaimed contemporary European painters and a master of the book as an art form.

D'Offay opened his travel bag and carefully unwrapped a beautifully bound book. It was a sketchbook that Kiefer had completed during the winter, spring, and summer of 1977, while living and working on the coast of Norway. The artist had painted watercolor illustrations of the land and sea and a series of erotic female nudes. The images took my breath away. I marveled at his colors—the deep blues and violets, reds and oranges. Kiefer is best known for his brooding forests and somber fields encrusted with debris and for his haunted monuments of the Nazi past.

D'Offay offered to sell me the sketchbook for $25,000. I said, "Tony, I don't have the $25,000, but I would be happy to publish a facsimile of the book." D'Offay said, "Well, George, I am shopping it around. If I don't sell it, we might have a talk." A few months later, D'Offay called to say he sold the sketchbook to U.S. Senator Heinz from Pennsylvania, who then donated the book to the Museum of Fine Arts in Boston.

I called Theodore E. Stebbins Jr., the senior curator at the museum, and convinced him to let me publish the facsimile edition. I told him the book would help introduce Kiefer to an American audience and help to establish his reputation.

A Book by Anselm Kiefer contains delicately executed watercolors, which reveal a wholly different side of the artist. This extraordinary art book, which includes a splendid introduction by Stebbins, demonstrates Kiefer's brilliant use of the book form as a means of artistic expression.

Dorothea Tanning

It sometimes happens in publishing that something wonderful and unexpected happens. You hope and wait for such moments. Such a moment came the day the artist Dorothea Tanning called, saying she wanted to meet with me to discuss publishing her work.

We met at Dorothea's studio at Fifth Avenue and 12th Street in Manhattan. I was struck by how lovely she was. She took my breath away—but that was almost everybody's natural reaction to Dorothea. After a few minutes of conversation, I listened as she outlined exactly what she had in mind.

She explained that she had been thinking about a book for fifty years. It would be the first comprehensive overview of her work. Lavishly illustrated with more than 200 color plates and containing lively critical essays, it would offer her assessment of figurative painting, the culmination of her lifelong commitment to romantic eroticism.

Sometimes publishers (like me) say yes without knowing what they are letting themselves in for, often changing their minds and deeply disappointing the writer or artist. I have done this a few times, thought I would finally learn, but never did. Luckily, however, I did not have to disappoint Dorothea.

After our meeting, I did what most editors would do: I checked to see if anything had been published about her. I spoke to one or two art critics, looked into potential costs and sales, and so forth. I soon learned that Dorothea was a genuinely unique figure in the international art world. As the art critic Donald Kuspit wrote, "[Tanning] is heir to the surrealist magic, the keeper of its uncompromising flame. Still urgently in pursuit of the marvelous, she comes up with pictures that are so purely fantasy that they can be read as allegorical personifications of the unconscious itself."

After many years in Paris, where she had lived with her husband, Max Ernst, Dorothea returned to New York in 1979. She lived there until her death in 2012.

In 1998, she sent me this letter, as we were planning the publication

of a second book, *Another Language of Flowers,* a collection of her artwork illustrated with poetry by James Merrill, Adrienne Rich, John Ashbery, Richard Howard, and others. Her letter gives the reader a small glimpse into the thoughtful, artistic sensibility with which she approached everything she did.

Dear George,

A muttering, growling, wet and lugubrious Monday, and you are probably out in your country hideaway while I am here chafing at this interminable weekend and eager to tell you some thoughts and show you a lovely surprise, at least I think you will be pleased.

You see, I have come around to your original wish to get Another Language of Flowers *out this fall. Our "presentation" ideas, though not without interest, surely should dictate the book's appearance and, moreover, will probably take shape when the time grows near. In the meantime, we can go ahead with production immediately.*

1. The "surprise," well, it is that I have ready for your perusal a complete dummy of the entire 64 pages (that is, 59, the last 5 to be decided). So that TR or whoever, can rip off a computerized film in no time.

2. All photographic material will be in my hands by the end of the week. And I would be happy to try your color printer. 12 color plates and 12 black and whites (the sketches for the paintings as per your suggestion—great!).

3. All textual matter is in, and integrated in the dummy, correctly spaced, etc. My machine used Palatino—you may want another font.

4. We should get together for the cover. After some tries I have come up with something pretty dramatic and eye-catching: a detail of the last painting (have you seen it?), entirely covering the front of the jacket with the TITLE superimposed, in hand script, maybe . . .

5. What remains is your meeting with the Academy people to discuss sponsorship—whether they will want to join in its publication—or whether you will want that.

Dear George, I hope this is readable, it's always easier to talk. But perhaps we can meet soon. Call me when you get this.

Fondly,

Dorothea
May 25, 1998

Architecture

I am often approached by young architects who speak with great enthusiasm about our Masters of World Architecture series. "Oh, Mr. Braziller, I grew up on those books," they say. "They meant so much to me."

They meant so much to me, too. These books were one of a kind. My editor, William Alex, almost singlehandedly commissioned and produced this series. Without him, we could not have created it.

The books' subjects are luminaries, an entire generation of significant mid-twentieth-century European and American architects: among them, Walter Gropius, founder of the Bauhaus School; Ludwig Mies Van der Rohe, innovator in glass-and-steel architecture; Louis Sullivan, the "father of skyscrapers"; and Frank Lloyd Wright, genius of organic architecture. The authors—their students—represent a new generation of influential architectural scholars and historians: Vincent Scully Jr., Ada Louise Huxtable, Albert Bush-Brown, and James Marston Fitch, to name just a few.

"Never before in this country has such a series been published," wrote one reviewer in the *New York Times Book Review,* "generously illustrated, written with high seriousness and intended not only for the professional architect and student, but also for the public at large."

The eleven groundbreaking books in this innovative series have shaped a new generation of architects and city planners. During the four years in which we produced them, I had no idea what a long-lasting effect they would have on lovers and students of architecture.

Hercules Segers

When does writing become a diary entry, or, if it comes to that, when does it become prose? I try to opt for prose. I struggled most of the morning with a piece for my memoirs. For whatever reason, I was not only stuck but sort of let down. I got up from my desk and walked into the kitchen, drank two glasses of water. I decided the best thing to do was to get out of the study and go to the Whitney Museum, which, although familiar, was always enjoyable to visit.

As a member of the Whitney, I was able to bypass the long line of visitors. I followed the crowd to the elevators, thinking they might know what was worth seeing. I exited with the crowd and went off on my own, scanning the works chosen by the Whitney for its biennial of "new" artists.

Suddenly I heard strange, intriguing music emanating from a room off to one side, curtained by long strips of heavy plastic, which muffled the music a bit. People were entering and leaving, and I decided to take a look at the goings-on. A documentary by filmmaker Werner Herzog was playing. The subject was the relatively unknown seventeenth-century Dutch artist Hercules Segers, a contemporary of Rembrandt. The spellbinding music, played by cellist Ernst Reijseger, filled the large room. People were seated reverently in the darkness on low box-like chairs. No one made a sound.

I had never seen or heard such an appropriate coming together of music and art as I felt in that room. Segers's landscapes, done in shades of brown, grey, and green, looked like cultivated farmlands recently plowed under and abandoned. I couldn't take my eyes from them. It was as though they were moonscapes. I whispered to myself, "Where are those images from?" Of course! The power of these landscapes reminded me of that of the landscapes of Vincent van Gogh.

These powerful, imaginative scenes—with the vastness of the imagery, which borders on abstraction—did not seem to me to be landscapes at all. They seemed to be, as Herzog's exhibit notes described, "states of mind—full of angst, desolation, solitude—a dreamlike vision."

Herzog likened Segers's paintings to a "hearsay of the soul," the title of the exhibit. "Segers signifies the beginning of modernity." He described the landscapes as "flashlights held in our uncertain hands."

Walking back to my apartment, I recalled the book on Segers that we had published in 1973—the very first book of the work of this extraordinary artist. Just as Segers was barely known, even to artists of his day, the book was barely noticed by the public. Oh, the beauty and power of art! I don't know how others reacted to the exhibit, but it was the most uplifting experience I had had all day.

One Hundred Famous Views of Edo

When *One Hundred Famous Views of Edo* by the Japanese painter and printmaker Hiroshige first appeared in the late nineteenth century, this set of 100 prints was celebrated in Japan. "It was clear from the start," wrote art historian Henry D. Smith III, "that the *One Hundred Famous Views of Edo* would be no ordinary series of landscape prints." Hiroshige introduced a striking new technique of composition, which involved setting large framing elements against a distant background. Combined with the superb printing and with the artist's proven skills at evocative depiction of landscape, this compositional inventiveness guaranteed the contemporary success of the work.

Hiroshige's series of prints became just as famous in the West—especially in France, where it caught van Gogh's attention. Van Gogh especially admired two of the prints, *Plum Estate* (Plate 30) and *Sudden Shower* (Plate 58). He made a copy of each one and credited each with the name Hiroshige.

I heard that the Brooklyn Museum had a complete collection, in mint condition, of all of the prints from *One Hundred Famous Views of Edo.* The Oriental Department recovered the set in 1970, through the efforts of Amy Poster, the associate curator. Of course, I was excited to hear about the Hiroshige prints and the possibility of publishing the set. My editors, Beatrice Rehl and Charles Miers, and I called on Amy Poster.

The next week, there we were at the Brooklyn Museum of Art: Rehl, Miers, Poster and I, looking in amazement at the first set of the original prints of *One Hundred Views.* The editors felt it would be a significant event for us to publish this remarkable series. As museum director Robert Buck wrote in his preface, "For the first time in the West, all of the images of this extraordinary series, one of the outstanding monuments of late Edo period print-making, can be seen together as a whole."

Greece

During the hot summer of 1994, I was island hopping alone in Greece. I set out to see the Gorge of Samaria in the White Mountains, in the southwestern part of the island of Crete. It is a place of awesome natural beauty. There are no roads in the gorge, only a trail two miles long. It is a two-hour walk to cover the entire distance, and it helps if you are a seasoned hiker—which I wasn't. A sign advises visitors: "Your hike through the gorge is a pilgrimage. Please respect, preserve, and appreciate."

Before entering the gorge, I registered at the patrol desk. I had to show a valid passport, give my age, declare whether I was traveling alone or with companions, show what supplies (especially water) I had brought along, and give a reasonable estimate of my state of health. The patrol officers were surprised when I gave my age (seveny-eight) and asked if I thought I could undertake what looks at first glance like a pleasant stroll. My sneakers and leisure clothing worried them. With not a drop of water in a knapsack, things didn't look too good.

I was beginning to have second thoughts about the entire venture. The patrol officer told me that there was a rest station halfway down the trail, and I was to wait there if I thought I needed help. With lingering doubts still nagging at me, I finally entered the trail.

The entrance to the gorge is at an altitude of about 2,000 feet. I envisioned a nice, gradual slope leading into the gorge, with a well-maintained footpath to stay on safely. Far from it! The trail was littered with boulders and rocks of every size and shape, providing very poor footing. It had taken many an earthquake to create so much rubble. As I walked, I never had both feet firmly on the ground at the same time. In no time all, I might expect a twisted ankle or worse. The drop into the gorge, from the moment I started on the trail, was terrifying.

I had only been walking for about twenty minutes when I stepped aside to observe a hiker, strapped to a donkey, being taken back to the entrance. I decided to return, too. As I looked up—seeing nothing but those damn boulders and the sky at a distance that seemed unattainable—I couldn't decide which was worse, continuing or returning. Either way, the

Which is the donkey?

effort would be daunting. I knew I couldn't make it and I was beginning to feel frightened.

Some hikers took me under their wing and helped me. I was determined to keep moving along with them whatever might happen. Two patrol guides then appeared, explaining they were looking for me. They gave me some water and lifted me up on a donkey for the exit trip out of the gorge. From the back of a donkey, the trail looked steeper than ever! I reminded myself not to look down and put all my trust in that little donkey. I held on to the reins for dear life.

That trusty little donkey never missed a step, in spite of the dangerous boulders along the trail. I didn't dare budge one inch to the left or right. I thought that if I fell I might never move again. When we arrived at the entrance to the gorge, I thanked everyone and gave the donkey a big kiss.

Ben Shahn

The American artist Ben Shahn was a witty raconteur, who could talk endlessly on any subject, mostly politics. Although I was not always in agreement with him, I loved the give-and-take conversation. His work always held a certain appeal for me. It was satirical, bitter, and compassionate. His paintings and graphics dealt with many of the social themes of the 1920s and 1930s—the Sacco and Vanzetti trial, the unemployed who stood on bread lines, the plight of farmers in the Dust Bowl.

A week after the assassination of President John F. Kennedy in 1963, Ben walked into my office unannounced. He handed me a sketchbook and asked if I would look at it. "George, what do you think of this?" He had been inspired by a poem entitled "November 26, 1963" which had run in *The Nation* magazine. The young poet, Wendell Berry, had written the poem out of grief in the days after the assassination.

> *we know the mouth of the grave waiting, the bugle and*
> *rifles, the mourners turning away;*
> *we know the young dead body carried in the earth into*
> *the first deep night of its absence...*

Shahn had illustrated the poem in his sketchbook. It didn't take me long to answer. I looked at the drawing, read the poem, and said I would publish them. Ben was surprised and pleased by my reaction.

In publishing, as in any business, it is important to get things in writing, but Ben wouldn't hear of a contract between us. He said a handshake was good enough for him, and it should be good enough for me. He assumed our mutual love for art and politics would see us through any differences that might arise.

After the successful publication of *November 26, 1963,* Ben suggested making a lithograph that I would publish in a limited edition of 200 signed and numbered copies. We began to discuss terms, and I suggested we put everything down on paper so there could be no doubt as to how to proceed with the project. Ben wouldn't hear of it. I still regret giving in to him.

Publishers traditionally pay artists and authors a royalty on the actual sales of prints and books. Ben, however, insisted that I pay him outright for the 200 prints upon delivery. His portion of the work was finished, he said, and he wanted to be compensated.

Ben was angry about our miscommunication, and we never met again. Some years later, when I heard that he was very ill, I called him and said that I wanted to see him to set things right. I was shattered when he said no. He died a couple of months later. This unfortunate incident is one of the few in my career that I look back upon with deep regret.

Anne Frank

During the cold and rainy month of November 1968, I visited my Dutch printer in Amsterdam—a city I love, a city with 165 canals and 1,300 bridges. I was there to oversee the printing of a forthcoming book that we were publishing.

One day, while I was still in Amsterdam, the name Anne Frank came suddenly to my mind. I wondered, "How could I not have thought of it before?" It would have been unconscionable to have been in Amsterdam and not visit the house where Anne Frank and her family hid from the Nazis.

The house, now a museum, is located at Prinsengracht 263-267. When I approached, I saw there was a line of visitors. I had to wait two hours to get in. I, like millions, have read *The Diary of Anne Frank,* which gives such a vivid and heartbreaking account of the years she and her family spent living in a "secret annex" to avoid capture by the Nazis who occupied Holland.

The rooms were small, and the hallways narrow. The house had been restored to what it had been like when the family lived there. I visited the windowless annex and almost broke down to see the conditions in which they had lived—both in terms of ventilation and sanitary conditions. There, Anne Frank, who aspired to be a journalist, kept a diary for two years. On April 5, 1944—four months before the family's capture—she wrote: "If I don't have the talent to write books or newspaper articles, I can always write for myself. But I want to achieve more than that."

As the writer Primo Levi, an Auschwitz survivor, said, "One single Anne Frank moves us more than the countless others who suffered just as she did but whose faces have remained in the shadows. Perhaps it is better that way; if we were capable of taking in all the suffering of all those people, we would not be able to live."

William Caxton's *Metamorphoses*

While in London in December 1967, I read in the *London Times* a story about an effort to raise £90,000 to save a rare and historic manuscript that had been purchased by an American book dealer. The book was volume one of Ovid's *Metamorphoses,* translated and printed in 1480 by William Caxton, England's first printer. The money had to be raised by February 1968—only two months away—or this important manuscript would leave England.

I thought about the story for a couple of days and then decided, Why not try to save the manuscript? It would bring prestige to our small publishing house—and, at the same time, it would save the manuscript for Merry Old England.

I went to the British Museum to see Sir Frank Francis, who was the chief librarian. He was also coordinating the museum's efforts to save the Caxton manuscript. He shared that responsibility with Ralph Bennett, a fellow at Magdalene College, Cambridge.

With some difficulty—and a little help from Sir Frank's secretary—I got past the guards and met Sir Frank in his office. He was a typical Englishman in his dress and his manner. He was polite and friendly and put me at ease at once. We talked about my stay in England and my visits to book publishers. He offered me tea, naturally. Then, cautiously, I mentioned my plan for saving the manuscript.

I said I would raise the money needed to save the manuscript. I would also reproduce a facsimile edition. I would assume complete responsibility for the production and sale of the book. Both Sir Frank and Bennett approved the plan, and I returned to New York.

I approached Eugene Power, a retired American businessman and the inventor of microfilm, a technology that helped make out-of-print books widely available to readers. Power had an interest in rare manuscripts and was grateful to the British Museum for giving him access to its collection. I explained my plan to Power, explained the urgency, and asked for his help. He agreed to give the museum an interest-free loan to purchase the manuscript.

With the proceeds from the sale of 1,200 copies of the facsimile edition, the loan was repaid. The Caxton manuscript is now where it belongs—in the Pepys Library, side by side with its companion volume.

I'm glad I took on the project, but all along I questioned whether I was being realistic. Without the money from Powers, I couldn't have done it. With the money, we fulfilled the plan, and it was a worthwhile effort.

Magdalene College honored both Eugene Powers and George Braziller Publishers at a celebration to mark the publication of the book. I had done my bit for Merry Old England.

Huffington Post

At noon on July 2, 2010, I began to receive phone calls and an email asking if I had seen the Huffington Post that day. I hadn't seen it, so I went to my computer and read as follows, a post written by Anis Shivani:

> *Three individuals—James Laughlin (New Directions, est. 1936), George Braziller (George Braziller, Inc., est. 1955), and Barney Rosset (Grove Press, est. 1951) stand out in the history of independent publishing in America and they should be the models for every striving young independent press. These three, more than others, were responsible for introducing a world awareness to American literature—they brought in radical new voices from abroad, and they never compromised the mission, never sold out, never reached for the easy formula and the cheap profit. Braziller—whose unfailing judgment brought us Claude Simon, Buchi Emeceta, Janet Frame, Alasdair Gray, Amin Maalouf, and Orhan Pamuk—is still going strong at 94.*

Pablo Picasso

One summer, Marsha and I were in Antibes, one of the most beautiful seaport cities in France. Our friend, the photographer Marianne Greenwood, was also there, shooting a photo essay on Picasso for the magazine *Photo*.

Marianne invited us to meet her at the Grimaldi Museum. The building had been Picasso's studio and home for six months during World War II. There we met the director, who invited us to walk through the collection of Picasso's paintings, most of which I had never seen. Anything I might have said about these great works would only have sounded banal, so I kept my mouth shut.

Soon after, the director invited us to have dinner with Picasso at the museum. I was flabbergasted. I turned to Marsha, who had that wonderful movement with her hands, not knowing what to say, but her face said it all.

When we met Picasso, we were surprised at how short he was and how graceful he was in his movements. He smoked constantly and talked with Marianne and the director in French. My own French was rather poor, but Marianne, who was fluent, translated, and we managed to get along. At dinner, we watched Picasso carve up the fish. He held up its bare bones by the tail to admire as a thing of beauty.

As the dinner ended, we all stood up quietly and faced the Mediterranean. Picasso said, "This is where I would like my studio to be." Then he turned and invited us to visit his home and studio.

The next day, Marianne, Marsha, and I called on Picasso and his wife, Jacqueline. Again with the help of Marianne as translator, I expressed our appreciation to Picasso and Jacqueline for welcoming us so kindly and showing us around the studio. There were paintings everywhere, in various stages of preparation. During our conversation, I told Picasso how much I admired him. We spoke about his painting *Guernica* and the impact he had had on my generation during the Spanish Civil War.

Picasso then asked me to tell him about the new artists of interest in America. Of course, I mentioned the obvious ones—Jackson Pollock,

Marsha, Picasso and myself

Willem de Kooning, and Mark Rothko—but I had difficulty saying all I wanted to say because of the language barrier.

After expressing our appreciation and saying good-bye to Picasso and his wife, Marsha and I left the house. Picasso waved to us as we walked down the hill. For a long time, Marsha and I walked in silence. Finally, we began to talk excitedly about how overwhelmed we were by Picasso's generosity and how fortunate we were to have spent so much time with this great artist.

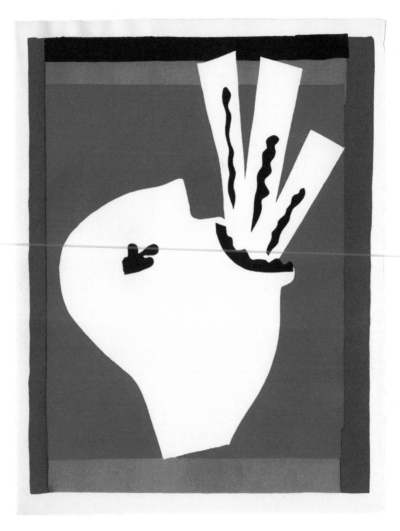

The Sword Swallower, Plate 13 from *Jazz.*

Henri Matisse's *Jazz*

What a great joy and privilege it was in 1983 to publish Henri Matisse's book *Jazz*—the French artist's paper cutout masterpiece—one of the great art books of the twentieth century.

I had always wanted to publish this magnificent book, first issued in a limited edition in 1947 by the French publisher Tériade. *Jazz* is an exquisite suite of twenty color plates and sixty-eight pages of text, which, like the music that inspired it, was created in a spirit of improvisation and spontaneity. This book falls into the rarest category of all: the book as a work of art.

I met with Tériade, a warm and witty man, in his little carriage-house office. I showed him a few examples of what Braziller had published, including Joan Miro's *À Toute Épreuve*. His polite smile told me that it was presumptuous of me to imagine I could duplicate the great work of his press. I knew he thought it would be impossible for anyone to do justice to the Matisse.

Tériade indulged me, but I could see that I was getting nowhere, even when I assured him that the proposed facsimile would be faithful to the book, down to the last thumbprint. Tériade finally said he would say yes if the Matisse family said yes. I was thrilled the day—three years later—that Pierre Matisse, the artist's son, finally gave me permission.

My editor, Charles Miers, and I visited Ernst Waltensteiner, the German printer in Munich whom I knew from my war years. We explained to him that it was very important that we match the quality of the original edition. He assured me the work would be done right—and it was. Charles stayed in Munich for a full week to oversee the printing while the book was on press.

This project called for the finest paper, the highest-quality printing, the best of everything. The costs were high, but I had such faith in the project—and felt so privileged to have the opportunity to realize the publication of such an extraordinary work of art—that I wasn't concerned about the costs.

As Riva Castleman, then the Museum of Modern Art's director of Prints and Illustrated Books, wrote in her introduction to the book:

With Jazz you hold an artist's spirit in your hands. Each page reveals deeply felt ideas, years of dedication to art and its craft, innate sensitivity to visual stimuli and their perfect organization for the most exhilarating, most satisfying result. Few artists have added to their pictorial work words that have been equally important in form and meaning. The precise equilibrium of these elements in Jazz is Matisse's unique achievement. The dark rhythms, roiling counterpoint, happy staccatos, and jolting dissonances of this Jazz will sound forever. Matisse has taught the eye to hear.

Matisse himself described the book as the "closest thing to an autobiography" he had ever created.

Cry Out: Poets Protest the War

On February 16, 2003, the Bush adminstration was preparing to launch the war against Iraq. Approximately five thousand American soldiers died and more than 32,000 were wounded in the war. It still breaks my heart to read those figures.

I traveled from New York to Vermont at the request of the poet and author Jay Parini. I must admit that only a poet like Parini could have gotten me to make such a long trip during that cold winter.

A group of contemporary poets were gathering for a poetry reading to honor the right to protest as a "patriotic and historical American tradition." The threat of war was once again hanging over us. Only a week before, I—like thousands of others marching along the grey streets of America—had protested the war in Iraq.

When I arrived, I was amazed to see that almost 800 people had jammed into the First Congregational Church in Manchester. All of these people had gathered to hear eleven poets read their poems and the poems of other poets not present.

Among the poets present—some of whose work I did not already know—were Julia Alvarez, Donald Hall, Jamaica Kincaid, Galway Kinnell, William O'Daly, Grace Paley, Jay Parini, and Ruth Stone.

A week later, after discussing the idea with my poetry editor, Richard Howard, I decided to publish the poems in a collection titled *Cry Out: Poets Protest the War*. The book also includes the poems of such poets as Langston Hughes, Pablo Neruda, and Walt Whitman.

Cry Out celebrates the role of poetry as a means of peaceful protest and reminds us that, although it might take time, as Parini wrote, "the language of poetry seeps through" and has the potential to redirect the fate of nations.

Richard Minsky

I often travel from New York City to visit my friends Richard Minsky and Barbara Slate in Hudson, New York. I always look forward to these visits. The train ride upstate to their home is an enjoyable two-hour ride along the river and the majestic Palisades. For some reason, on every trip it seems I have some kind of incident. On one occasion I fell asleep and went past my station. Another time I refused to hand over my train ticket because I didn't have a seat and got into an argument with the conductor. On another trip, I was reading *War and Peace* for the first time and got so excited I started reading some of the pages out loud, until one of the other passengers finally told me to shut up.

On one of my visits, Richard asked me to come into his studio so he could show me a project he had been working on. Richard is a renowned book artist and book collector, scholar and curator. His two-room studio looked as though a cyclone had passed through. One room was full of his bookbinding equipment—hand tools, paper cutters, binding machines, printing presses, computers, inking machines. I was always amazed that he was able to find whatever he was looking for.

The other room was pristine. Enclosed in glass cases was his book collection—beautifully crafted volumes by some of the most important book designers of the late nineteenth and early twentieth centuries. Richard talked about his collection and the historical and artistic significance of these books. As I listened and watched him work, I thought about how extraordinary these covers were as art and, naturally, began to think of publication.

Out of this visit came the remarkable book called *The Art of American Book Covers: 1875–1930*. Richard wrote the introduction and the text, which presents an overview of historical book design and technology, trends, and influences on contemporary book artists. The book contains more than 100 color plates and details of volumes in his collection—examples of some of the finest books from the Golden Age of American book art, when publishers revered book covers as works of art.

Selected covers from *The Art of American Book Covers: 1875-1930*

Norman Rosten

It's nice to recall a writer like Norman Rosten—author, playwright and poet, whom I met for the first time in the mid '40s. I was something of an innocent; I was about thirty. But he completely won me over by his dynamic personality, his infectious wit.

Over the many years, we became close friends. Norman was the kind of writer who gave thought to everything about life—the good and bad—with such passion he would have you believe that there was nothing wrong with the world.

As his publisher, I was glad that he was named poet laureate of Brooklyn in 1979 and received an award from the Academy of Arts and Letters in recognition of his work for poetry. Brooklyn proved to be an inspiration to Rosten and in his writings he captured the vitality and complexities of its varried communities. It is astonishing that during Rosten's long writing career he wrote more than ten volumes of poetry, three novels and ten plays. Thinking of him and his work, I smile and can still recall my years of growing up in Brooklyn, its joys and sorrows.

A little about gossip. Norman had something of a reputation as a womanizer. When he was writing a book called *Marilyn: An Untold Story* and a long poem entitled "For Marilyn Monroe," it was rumored that they were having an affair. I completely believed him when he said to me: "Not true." It would be ironic if Norman is remembered primarily for his slim book about Marilyn Monroe.

What stands out for me and should be long remembered of Rosten's many writings is his masterpiece: *The Selected Poems of Norman Rosten.*

Photo by Charles Forberg

Jim's Painting

For the past fifty years, I have been looking at this painting, done by my son, Jimmy, when he was eight years old. Today, as I work on my memoir, I am inspired to write about it. What was there about it that held my attention?

In the summer of 1951, the family—Marsha, Michael, Jimmy, and I—were spending the summer in Menemsha, Martha's Vineyard, in a yellow box house we had rented. It was a hot August day, and we decided to head for the beach. Jimmy said he didn't want to go swimming and asked if he could use my easel to do some painting. (At the time, I was dabbling in art.) Of course I said okay and set him up with paints and brushes.

When we returned later that afternoon, Jimmy had completed this painting. I was amazed at how good it was. It is exactly as you see it here: the vivid colors, the composition, the shape and form of the vase, the white of the canvas outlining the shapes. I grabbed him and hugged him and told him how good I thought it was. "Dad," he said, "I don't know how to close the colors." Our friend, the artist Bob Rosenwald, who had dropped by to visit, was there, too. He said, "Jim, leave it exactly the way it is. That's what makes the painting."

What a nice summer day that was!

Golf

I first learned the game of golf at the age of ten when I was working as a caddy at the Huntington Halesite Golf Club. I enjoyed watching the golfers play and walking on the fairways. I never quite understood why I was being paid ($1 for eighteen holes). On Mondays, we caddies were allowed to play for free, using the members' golf clubs. My caddying days ended when I was about sixteen, when my mother and I left Huntington and moved back to Brooklyn.

It was only after the war, in the 1950s, that I took up the game of golf again. I played on weekends with passion and love. I can even boast that I played a fairly good game. But the highlight came at the age of eighty, when I shot my first hole-in-one.

My visiting friends woke up to see this note:

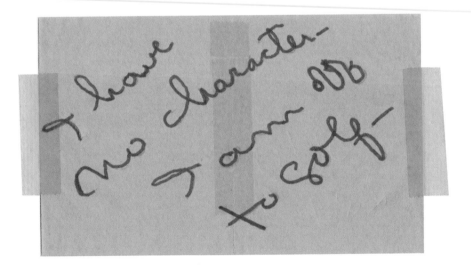

"The Tyranny of Time"

During the sparkling spring of 2011, after many twists and turns and trepidations, I decided to turn over the publishing house that I ran for fifty-six rewarding and interesting and difficult years to my two sons: Jim and Michael.

While it was a bold step, I felt that it was time for me to move on. My age of ninety-four and a series of medical problems limited the activities so necessary for my kind of work. After a series of talks with my sons about carrying on with the publishing house, I felt comfortable. Our dependable managing editor, Maxwell Heller, who had been with us for many years, agreed to work with them during the transition period.

Michael, to his credit, started in 1975 and runs with Karen Braziller Persea Books, their own small literary publishing house publishing poetry and literary works. He is now also the Editor and President of George Braziller, Inc.

Jim, who is an attorney in New York, has also assumed responsibilities at the publishing house.

Dialogue

Every so often, I go along courageously writing my memoir. Other times, I feel utter despair and wonder how good it is. So, again, I turn to my friends and try to elicit an honest comment and, of course, get mixed reactions and advice.

One day, while reading a favorite book of mine, *Specimen Days* by Walt Whitman, I came across this anecdote. On page 184, Whitman writes about taking a two-hour walk on the Commons in Cambridge, Massachusetts with his friend Ralph Waldo Emerson. Reflecting on that long walk, Whitman says about Emerson, "he was the talker and I the listener." It seems that Emerson was critical of Whitman's controversial poem, "Children of Adam," which had sexual overtones. Whitman agreed that Emerson was correct: "No judge's charge ever more complete or convincing." Yet, Whitman says, "I felt down in my soul the clear and unmistakable conviction to disobey all, and pursue my own way."

I was curious about their argument and decided to read Whitman's poem and include lines from it here:

Amorous, mature, all beautiful to me, all wondrous,
My limbs and the quivering fire that ever plays through them,
for reasons, most wondrous,
Existing I peer and penetrate still,
Content with the present, content with the past,
By my side or back of me Eve following,
Or in front, and I following her just the same.

Oh, Walt. You are so right. During these past three years, I have learned: If you want to make friends or want to lose them, write a memoir.

Diderot

The French philosopher and novelist Denis Diderot has been a favorite of mine ever since I published Elizabeth De Fontaney's book *Diderot: Reason and Resonance*. According to the *New York Times,* today—October 5, 2013—marks the 300th anniversary of Diderot's birth. The French president François Hollande announced that all of France would celebrate the symbolic reburial of Diderot's body in the Pantheon.

In an op-ed piece for the *Times,* Andrew S. Curran wrote, quoting Hollande, "'Like many Enlightenment writers,' Hollande said, 'Diderot preached the right of the individual to determine the course of his or her life.'" Diderot is remembered primarily for two things, Curran notes: coediting the world's first comprehensive encyclopedia and "being a scandalous freethinker and an atheist."

So, Braziller, what will you be remembered for? To be remembered for what I have believed in for these past ninety-eight years: the need to confront the world as it is, good and bad, and to try to bring some joy and happiness to it. I believe religion is far too biased, and I don't believe in God. Paraphrasing Bertrand Russell's lecture, "Why I Am Not a Christian," I must ask, "If there is a God, who made him?"

I do not fear death, as I know that sooner or later it comes to all of us. Also, I have instructed that, when I die, my body be turned over to science. Knowing that I will be helping someone else, bringing them health and happiness, fills me with joy.

Happy birthday, Diderot, from one atheist to another. I am sure your other fans—Goethe, Hegel, Freud, Marx, and Nietzsche—are raising a toast as well, wherever they are.

Looking Back

I find myself looking over and over again at this early photograph of myself at the age of twelve. I surprise myself when I say, "I love that boy." Suddenly I have a rush of warm feeling and bring the photo closer. I think very hard, as I look at it again, and wonder how he got so far as to reach the age of ninety-eight. The boy looks so pleased with himself, so at ease. He also looks like he is expecting to be asked something.

"All right, how did you get as far as you have?"

"Well, to be honest, I did it pretty much on my own—but not without the support of my colleagues."

Acknowledgments

I wish to thank Barbara Slate and Richard Minsky, whose idea it was that I tell my story and who kept after me for three years, offering helpful advice to see me through.

My sincere appreciation and thanks go to Vincent Torre for his essential editorial direction and for suggesting the final structure of the book.

To Amy Braziller, who set aside finishing her own book to provide me with crucial observations about the text, thank you, dear Amy.

I am also indebted to Deborah Cannarella, who came at a critical time, when I was completely lost in my writing, and who took away hundreds of yellow-lined pages and notes and with her understanding and editorial expertise, helped me bring the book to life.

Much love goes to the late Herbert Mitgang and to Shirley Mitgang for the many invaluable suggestions and advice they provided during the past three years.

My sincere thanks go to Adrienne Baxter Bell, who was kind enough to review the manuscript in its early stages and whose thoughtful suggestions encouraged me to continue writing.

To Nena Tsouti-Schillinger, who patiently listened to my stories over the years and who, with her expert advice, helped guide me over the finish line, I give my sincere thanks.

My thanks go to Larry List, who often dropped by with pizzas and gave me the support I very much needed.

My thanks also go to my son, Jimmy, for suggestions and fact-checking.

Credits

Grateful acknowledgment is made to the collection of George Braziller for the photograph of George Braziller on the cover, the photograph of the author's parents on page 12, the photograph of the author and a black Buick on page 24, the photograph of Marsha Braziller on page 30, the photograph of the cover of the *133d AAA Gun Battalion* on page 44, the photograph of the author in the Army at Cherbourg, France, on page 46, for the photograph of the author at the Frankfurt Book Fair on page 55, the photograph of Marilyn Monroe on page 62, the photograph of Janet Frame with the author on page 69, the image of "Pretty Diane" poem (poet unknown) on page 70, the photograph of Alessandra Comini and the author on page 91, the handwritten note by the author about Samuel Menashe on page 101, the photographs of George Braziller (photograph on the right by Maxwell Heller) on page 106, the photograph of Dorothea Tanning and the author on page 113, the photograph of the author on page 121, the image of the painting by Jim Braziller on page 138, the handwritten note by the author on page 140, the photograph of the author on page 141, and the photograph of the author as a young boy on page 145; to Gloria Norris Pomeranz for the frontispiece photograph; for the photographs of Huntington Station on page 20 and the author's school in Huntington, New York, on page 22 from *Portrait of a Small Town*, by Alfred V. Sforza; to Betsy Figatner for the photograph of Herman Figatner and the author on page 35; to a U.S. Army photographer for the photograph of the 133d AAA Gun Battalion on page 38; to Cynthia Hollingworth for the George Braziller, Inc., logo on page 48; to George Braziller, Inc., for cover image of *The Tale of Genji*, by Miyeko Murase on page 57, the publicity image for The Great American Artists Series on page 58, for the image from *The Hours of Catherine of Cleves*, by John Plummer on page 67, for the quotation from "Elementary Cosmogony" by Charles Simic from his *Selected Early Poems* on page 73, for cover image of *A Toute Épreuve*, art by Joan Miró and poems by Paul Eluard, on page 75, Miró image © Successió Miró/ Artists Rights Society (ARS), New York/ ADAGP, Paris 2015, for image of an etching by Rembrandt from *Great Drawings of the Louvre Museum*, by Maurice Serullaz and Roseline Bacou on page 87, for image of the cover of *The White Castle*, by Orhan Pamuk on page 89, for the image by Antonio Frasconi, poetry by Langston Hughes from *Let America Be America Again* on page 93, for image of the cover of *Einstein's 1912 Manuscript on the Special Theory of Relativity* on page 94, for image of the cover of *Ambrogio Lorenzetti, The Palazzo Pubblico, Siena*, by Randolph Starn on page 103, for image of the cover of *Daphnis and Chloe*, by Marc Chagall on page 109, Marc Chagall image © 2015 Artists Rights Society (ARS), New York/ ADAGP, Paris, for the cover image from *Hercules Segers,* by John Rowlands on page 117, for print by Hiroshige from *The 100 Famous Views of Ido*, by Henry D. Smith and Ando Hiroshige on page 118, for cover image of *November Twenty Six Nineteen Hundred Sixty Three*, art by Ben Shahn, poetry by Wendell Berry, on page 123, for image of the "The Sword Swallower" by Henri Matisse, from *Jazz*, on page 130, © 2015 Sucession H. Matisse/Artists Rights Society (ARS), New York; and for image of selected book covers from *The Art of American Book Covers: 1875-1930*, by Richard Minsky on page 135, all reprinted courtesy of the publisher; to Carl Hanser Verlag, Publishers, for the photograph of Michael Kruger on page 64; to Raymond Sarraute for the photograph of Nathalie Sarraute on page 77; to Ronald Glasser for the photograph of Ronald Glasser on page 81; to Elena Barnet for the photograph of Will Barnet on page 97; to The Nation for the quotation from "November 26, 1963," by Wendell Berry on page 122, reprinted courtesy of The Nation; to the Pepys Library for the image from *William Caxton's Metamorphoses* on page 126; to Marianne Greenwood for the photograph of Marsha Braziller, Picasso, and the author on page 129; and to Charles Forberg for the photograph of Norman Rosten on page 137.